THE KING GOD DIDN'T SAVE

Also by JOHN A. WILLIAMS

Novels

THE ANGRY ONES
NIGHT SONG
SISSIE
THE MAN WHO CRIED I AM
SONS OF DARKNESS, SONS OF LIGHT

Nonfiction

AFRICA: HER HISTORY, LANDS AND PEOPLE
THE PROTECTORS (With H. J. Anslinger)
THIS IS MY COUNTRY TOO
THE MOST NATIVE OF SONS
THE KING GOD DIDN'T SAVE

Reflections on the Life and Death

of

Martin Luther King, Jr.

The King
God Didn't Save

by JOHN A. WILLIAMS

Coward-McCann, Inc.
New York

Respectfully dedicated
to the memory of the man
Martin Luther King
could have become, had he lived.

I am deeply indebted to many people—named and unnamed—in all parts of the United States and in parts of Europe who helped make this book possible not only by sharing their views and providing information, but in many cases by reading the typescript as well. I am especially indebted to the staff of Mugar Memorial Library, Boston University.

Make no mistake ... they are going to come at you with words about democracy; you are going to be pinned to the wall and warned about decency; plump-faced men will mumble academic phrases ... gentlemen of the cloth will speak unctuously of values and standards; in short, a barrage of concentrated arguments will be hurled at you to temper the pace and drive of your movement....

Richard Wright
Black Power, 1954

Acknowledgments

For permission to reprint copyrighted material, the author also wishes to thank the following:

Arlington House for excerpts from *House Divided: The Life and Legacy of Martin Luther King* by Lionel Lokos, published by Arlington House, Inc., 1968, copyright © 1968 by Arlington House, New Rochelle, New York, used with permission; P. F. Collier, Inc., for excerpts from *Black Bourgeoisie: The Rise of a New Middle Class in the United States* by E. Franklin Frazier, published by P. F. Collier, Inc., 1962, copyright © 1962 by E. Franklin Frazier, reprinted by permission of the publisher; The Dial Press, Inc., for excerpts from *The Great White Hope* by Howard Sackler, published by The Dial Press in 1968, copyright © 1968 by Howard Sackler; The Dial Press, Inc., for excerpts from *Die, Nigger, Die!* by H. Rap Brown, published by The Dial Press in 1969, copyright © 1969 by H. Rap Brown, reprinted by permission of the publisher; Grove Press, Inc., for excerpts from *Sammy Younge, Jr.* by James Forman, published by Grove Press, Inc., copyright © 1968 by James Forman, reprinted by permission of the publisher; Harper & Row, Publishers, Inc., for excerpts from *Stride Toward Freedom* by Martin Luther King, Jr., published by Harper & Row, Publishers, Inc. 1958, *Where Do We Go from Here: Chaos or Community* by Martin Luther King, Jr., published by Harper & Row, Publishers, Inc., 1967, *Why We Can't Wait* by Martin Luther King, Jr., published by Harper & Row, Publishers, Inc., 1964, reprinted by permission of the publishers; Harper & Row, Publishers, Inc., for excerpts from *The Negro Revolt* by Louis Lomax, published by Harper & Row, Publishers, Inc., 1965, reprinted by permission of the publishers; Holloway House, Inc., for excerpts from *To Kill a Black Man* by Louis Lomax, published by Holloway House, Inc., 1968, copyright © 1968, by Louis Lomax, reprinted by permission of the publisher; Mr. Earl Mazo for permission to excerpt from his correspondence with the late Dr. Martin Luther King, Jr.; The Mugar Memorial Library of Boston University, for permission to quote from the collected papers of

14   ACKNOWLEDGMENTS

Dr. Martin Luther King, Jr.; Weybright and Talley, Inc., Publishers, for excerpts from *Martin Luther King, Jr.: His Life, Martyrdom and Meaning for the World* by William Robert Miller, published by Weybright and Talley, Inc., Publishers, 1968, copyright © 1968 by William Robert Miller, reprinted by permission of the author and publishers Weybright and Talley, Inc., New York; World Publishing Company and The New American Library for excerpts from *This Is My Country Too* by John A. Williams, published by The World Publishing Company and The New American Library, 1965, copyright © 1965 by John A. Williams, reprinted by permission of The World Publishing Company, Inc., a N.A.L. book.

The author also wishes to express his indebtedness to Mrs. Coretta Scott King for her permission to quote a passage from a letter to Chief Albert Luthuli written by her late husband, Dr. Martin Luther King, Jr., as collected at The Mugar Memorial Library of Boston University, and passages from Dr. King's doctoral dissertation published by University Microfilms, Inc.

Part One

THE PUBLIC MAN

One

THIS is a study of a man who died ahead of his time. He was a black man and in this nation he was *supposed* to die before his time. But, I mean, he died even *before* then.

This is a study of Martin Luther King, Jr., a unique man in many ways, but it is also a study of the awesome exercise of white power in the United States, and it was this power, finally, that cut King down in conspiracy, and then conspired to plug the memory of the man with putty.

What is white power? It is the efforts, successful so far, of established institutions to maintain the racial status quo, which means that white shall be exalted and all other colors shall not. White power is the press, the government, the courts, the schools, the colleges, the mercantile and industrial corporations; it is the labor unions, the churches. White power is like a marsh underfoot for anyone not white; it is treacherous and deadly. Martin Luther King came to this fearful recognition very late in a career that was all too brief, but the evidence abounds that, as James Meredith said, "King's killing was the best-timed one [for black people] in this century, because it resulted in maximum possible continuance of what he was trying to do. He was on his last legs. If he'd carried on with his planned Poor People's March, which he'd contemplated not doing, as a result of what was not happening, he could have gone the route of Marcus Garvey or others of the past. This is what this civilization has calculated for the Kings, but his death broke the cycle."

King's death was imminent. A tornado, springing out of the volatile weather conditions, bounced and reeled and shrieked through Memphis, Tennessee, spreading that city's garbage—uncollected for weeks now—through the streets and alleyways. Then the rain came, graying the heavens even more, and fastening a turbulent and grim aspect upon a city already locked in murderous racial tension. The rain fell steadily, pelting the roof of the Lorraine Motel—that same motel where plans for the Meredith March had been set—with nervous, drumming fingers, as if waiting, as if impatient.

Inside the motel, King was preparing to go to the Clayton Temple on Mason Street to address 2,000 people who were concerned about or directly involved in the city's garbage strike. The garbage workers were mostly black. King would talk about the necessity for nonviolent solutions to this latest racial crisis.

For violence had charged the air as electric storms hover in thunderheads. Only one additional act of mindlessness on the part of the dominating whites or the sick-and-tired blacks was required to loose the lightning bolts. Martin King knew it. There had already been incidents. He knew it when he leaned forward to speak to the audience that night. He was very tired. He had been traveling, drumming up interest in his Poor People's March scheduled for Washington, April 22. He had detoured to Memphis to quench the impending violence, and to utilize the situation to the advantage of the PPM. The press had been treating King with kid gloves.

For almost a year King had been more or less hinting in public that the alternative to his philosophy could only be violence. He had not gained the victories he needed to weaken the growing press-manufactured power and publicity of the "black militants." He had spoken out in condemnation of the Vietnam War; he had excoriated the institutions that constitute the white power structure, while publicly refusing to acknowledge the validity of black power. Martin King, the

Negro leader, was at crisis point, looking ahead to Washington. But in his closing remarks at Clayton Temple he spoke of death. Some have called this a premonition, but King always spoke of death, as if some primeval instinct within him knew that this was the ultimate and inevitable punishment for daring to challenge white power. He said, "Well, I don't know what will happen now. We've got some difficult days ahead. But it doesn't matter with me now. Because I've been to the mountaintop."

Twenty-four hours later, as if called once too often, death came and led Martin King back to the mountaintop.

Like nearly everyone else I knew, I was shaken with a powerful combination of grief and anger; *rage* is the word. I didn't know King and, in fact, had extensive reservations about his philosophy of nonviolence. I'd come to like him better when he came out in opposition to the Vietnam War. I could have liked him when he blasted America's clergymen from Albany, Georgia, and Birmingham, except that, being a clergyman, he should have known what other clergymen were like. My grief was based on what had happened, what *was* happening, what was in the offing for all black people. Whites, driven to conceal the lies by which they live, had created, so the phrase goes, the climate for murder. As a spider spins out its web, so America had spun out the brutal destiny of Martin King. My anger came at the newest display of white cowardice. The record will show that white people seldom attacked black people who were armed, but preyed upon the nonviolent with a hatred that can only be described as sick.

Within moments of his collapse on his hotel balcony, the American press flashed around the world the news of King's killing. That was fitting, for the press had helped to create King; it helps to create—and destroy—every public man.

As King lay dead, a great and joyful tremor ran underground in white America, muted only by the knowledge that public displays of such emotion were not in good taste. White people by and large still do not know what the other white guy is thinking, whether he is a "liberal" or not, and this, too, held in check any untoward display of joy. Also, Fascist-leaning Americans, racist-thinking Americans, have great reluctance to reveal themselves except in like company. Further, it was not quite the right time for most whites to indicate how they really felt about King and the Black Revolution. But one realtor in a Montana town immediately placed a sign in his window which read IT'S ABOUT TIME.

Those three words, coming when they did, just about summed up the sinister side of America.

Because I am a black man, white America linked me, as it did every other Negro in this nation to what Martin King said, did, wrote, and thought. And why not? Nothing would suit white people better than to believe that "22,000,000" black people, descendants of the enslaved, who had been exploited, segregated, brutalized, and murdered on whim, after almost half a thousand years of such treatment, were forgiving and committed to nonviolent change. America first shuddered, then rose in unison, it appears, when it confronted the reality in the last two years of King's life, that not every man was going to or *ever* had believed in turning the other cheek.

As King himself said often enough, nonviolence was designed to appeal to the conscience of a moral society. But long, long before his death, he must have known what every black person learns as a child: The white citizens of this nation, the overwhelming majority of them, live by few of their cherished moral precepts. Even among themselves they haven't practiced what they preached to one another. A man as intelligent as King had to know this because the most unlettered black dropout knows it. The stench of the American truth in which Jesus Christ and Patriotism are the handles to our deeds had to penetrate even the idealism of Martin King. He fought disillusionment. He fought the good fight, which always means that in the end you lose.

The day after his death I was walking across Columbus Circle with an old friend, Peter Winkler, a television cameraman I'd walked with in Nigeria and Spain. Pete was a refugee from Germany who got out of that country by joining the French Foreign Legion. His family had been destroyed by the Nazis. I recall that he treated me with a special quality of gentleness that day. As we passed in front of the Coliseum, one of two cops who were there, both wearing instead of a precinct number on their collars, the letter *B*, approached us. His eyes were puffed, and a beard was beginning to appear on his face. Undoubtedly, he had been pulling double shifts to help keep New York cool. The city was unreal during those days. The atmosphere was one of pervasive sadness and apprehension. Lindsay had gone on his walking tours in the ghettos; the police and firemen were on twenty-four hour alert. Sections of half a hundred cities around the nation were in flames.

The cop saluted me and said, "I'm sorry about Dr. King."

"Thank you," I said. I didn't know what else to say.

"Black people have to get the opportunity to express their dignity," he said. "It's got to happen soon."

I nodded in agreement. He chatted on while his partner stood aside; Pete had moved back a step or two. I kept thinking that Martin King's death was not worth a salute and polite conversation with a cop. Finally I told him that I had to go, and he went out into the street and halted traffic, which was going with the light, so Pete and I could cross.

That evening I appeared on New York's Channel 13 for a hastily called talk show that had as its theme, *Where Do We Go From Here?* Dr. Benjamin Spock, Congressman James Scheuer (one of the many candidates for Mayor of New York in 1969), Dr. Alvin F. Poussaint, and I sat around a table. The small studio was unusually tense and still; I'd done other shows there when the cameramen and assistants, the producers and their aides, were a large happy, joking family. Not so that night. Poussaint seemed unusually reflective and tense; Spock was shaken but forceful; Scheuer repeatedly commented on the "good white people," and how they would finish King's task, or words to that effect. I disagreed with him. We kept bouncing it around until our time was up and none of us knew where we were going from there.

When we broke, James Farmer, now an assistant to the Secretary of Health, Education, and Welfare, rose out of the shadows and we exchanged greetings; I hadn't seen him to speak to since Nigeria, 1965. One of the producers called me over and told me that there had been many calls from viewers, and one lady had complained that Dr. Spock had been on the side of the blacks. During the show Spock had said that if white people wanted a taste of what black people have to endure, they ought to go on a peace march and get hit with the police clubs, be the butt of police curses and be imprisoned.

I walked with Dr. and Mrs. Spock to the corner; we moved slowly in the warm spring night, and perhaps the fact that it was spring made the grief all the more cutting. We tend to hope anew in spring. They took a bus at the corner; I walked on to Grand Central to take a subway. That night I would not get involved with a white cab driver who would refuse to stop or whose cab I'd have to run after and catch at a red light. By that time many of the cabbies were moonlighting cops who were just as bad, if not worse than the cabbies themselves. But that night I knew I'd have the driver—cabbie or cop—out into the roadway if he looked like he didn't want to ride me; we'd just be out there throwing knuckles or stomping or something. So I took the subway.

Along with millions of others, I watched the funeral on television. The proceedings were disgustingly discreet, boringly low-keyed. King was a Baptist, and while his studies of Tillich, Wieman, Nietzsche, Hegel, and others may have made him appear an intellectual, he remained a Southern Negro Baptist minister. I suspect he didn't have a choice. When the will is there, Baptists are known to rock a church; soul drips from the ceiling and boogaloos from the pews. I wanted there to be wailing and gnashing of teeth; I wanted the choir to howl through "Nearer My God to Thee" or "Were You There When They Crucified My Lord?," with each chorus wrenching the heart more. I longed to see the black and white notables flee the pews, deeply moved as only black people singing spirituals can move listeners.

Instead I watched a "white" funeral in which Mrs. Martin Luther King, Jr., was as noble and steadfast as Mrs. John F. Kennedy had been. And I thought, sipping my vodka martini on the rocks, this is not *it*. The soul was gone; the justifiable anger was absent. There should have been anger; Sherman had far less provocation to burn the city than the black people of Atlanta in 1968, where visitors to the funeral were insulted by local whites. Atlanta was home to generations of Kings, but it remained standing. Yet away from Atlanta a tornado of black rage and anger burned a swath across the nation to within blocks of the Capitol and the White House, which had to be secured with troops.

It was clear that those rebelling, vengeance-seeking blacks were thinking: If this can happen to the best of us, what's the fate for the least of us? Martin King was "another man done gone," another on the list of nameless slaves, chain-gang prisoners; he was another Mack Parker, Emmett Till, James Chaney, and Sammy Younge; and yes, he was James Reeb, and Goodman and Schwerner who, although white, died the death of black men deep in the South, at night, overpowered by men with weapons, large numbers of men, including the local law enforcement officials.

So now the man is dead, and time is already proving that his philosophy began to die before he did. "We Shall Overcome," practically discarded as the movement anthem during the final year and a half of King's life, is now sung by European students as they revolt; Arab women have been reported singing it in Israel; Catholics in Northern Ireland sing it as they march through crowds of hostile Protestants. White groups in America that were at the most tepid about King, now sing it when they troop in protest against some issue having nothing to do with race.

I hear the song now; hear King's voice rising from the deepest recesses of his lungs, his lips parted, his slanted eyes fixed in concentration; I hear Ralph Abernathy pumping over the bridge of the song between "day" and "deep," seeking the high note as he always did.

The song is now all but discarded, not because black people no longer seek to overcome, but because the time for singing is past.

Two

THE United States Supreme Court on May 17, 1954, issued what used to be called a historic ruling against segregated schools. Immediately the press predicted another Civil War. The rednecks and crackers and soft-drawling Southern Bourbons spoke of murder instead of compliance (today when they holler about law and order, they mean murder, as usual). Cooler heads hoped that it would be possible to avoid bloodshed; that the cracks in the system could somehow be sealed. Instead, what was uncovered were fissures running deep into the North—to the delight of the crackers who always knew they did, anyway.

The symbol of white power at this time was one Dwight D. Eisenhower, a former general of the Army, Columbia University president and golfer. Eisenhower was privately upset by what Chief Justice Warren's court had brought in. He did not know that during that same month a young, black graduate student, a candidate for the degree of Doctor of Philosophy at Boston University who had done his undergraduate work at Morehouse (1948) and secured his Bachelor of Divinity degree at Crozer Theological Seminary (1951), had preached his first sermon as the minister of the Dexter Avenue Baptist Church in Montgomery.

Martin King had been a good student—even, some say, brilliant. He was extremely self-possessed, and his abilities as a speaker were unquestioned. He was something of a clothes-horse, standing out even on the Morehouse College campus where sartorial splendor was something of a norm. No one could deny that he was a serious young man; at the same time, he had a marvelous sense of humor and the quick wit that is so much a part of young black men who love to engage in black repartee. Sometimes it was difficult to glimpse the somber minister in the suave King.

In September, 1954, King and his wife Coretta, whom he had met in Boston while he was studying at the seminary there, moved to Montgomery. The marriage had ended rumors that young King was originally to have married someone else in Atlanta, and later someone in Philadelphia.

Throughout that fall the South was in a slow, bitter boil. Southern Congressmen rarely appeared in the press without voicing the mumbo jumbo of "interposition," the vague doctrine that gives individual states the right to oppose any federal action that infringes on their powers. Less than a century before, the South had commenced a war because the North "meddled" in its affairs.

King had refused offers to pastor churches in the North, but had returned South because he and Coretta said that they "had something of a moral obligation to return—at least for a few years." He would "satisfy [his] fondness for scholarship later by turning to the teaching field." His doctoral dissertation, *A Comparison of God in the Thinking of Paul Tillich and Henry Nelson Wieman,* does indicate that he leaned more toward systematic theology than preaching. One of his professors at Boston University told me that it was still King's hope, late in his career, to leave public life and get back to his studies.

So now he was back, the idea of studies behind him, the "moral obligation" ready to be fulfilled. As fall eased into winter, white tempers that had flared over some tentative attempts by blacks to integrate, still burned at the indignity. But black people have tempers too, and in Montgomery they lost them.

Race made news in 1954 and 1955; it moved from the back

pages of the newspapers to the headlines. On television, which was still trying to break away from patterns set by radio, the Montgomery boycott became the biggest show going, and the show's star, Martin King, was a natural for the part.

You heard talk in the black communities that "that cat who was leading the boycott was 'Heavy, man, *heavy.*' " "Had gone to Harvard." "Was a doctor something or other." "Brilliant, baby." The press was more accurate. While at Crozer he was a graduate student in the philosophy department at the University of Pennsylvania, and while at Boston working toward a degree in systematic theology, he was a special student in the philosophy department at Harvard. As a junior at Morehouse in 1947, he was ordained by his father, and in his father's church, Ebenezer Baptist in Atlanta, and he was assistant pastor there for two years and copastor for four.

King was not one of those oldtime Baptist ministers, still to be found in many black churches. No fire and brimstone from him. Indeed, he was often accused of talking down to his congregations. For example, he often tried to explain what *agape* was, a kind of love he had explored in his doctoral thesis: "*Agape* affirms the other unconditionally. It is *agape* that suffers and forgives. It seeks the personal fulfillment of the other." King's father was reported to have told him after such a sermon that he should preach and not teach. But young King was not too "high flown" for the press; its representatives liked him.

Like nearly everyone else, I followed the progress of the Montgomery boycott. Reporting for the New York *Post* were Ted Poston and Murray Kempton, two writers whose innate sympathies were obvious. Wayne Phillips handled the early coverage for the New York *Times*. At the beginning, the boycott was featured almost every night in the news slots, and an abundance of television "specials" were devoted to it. The boycott drew sympathy and money from around the world. The idea that the protest was nonviolent immediately made the blacks the underdogs. (Indeed, had they ever been anything else?) It seems incredible now. But then there was an air of sympathy, of hope, of the possibility of a racial breakthrough to better times.

Louis E. Lomax, whose family hailed from rural Georgia, who grew up with King, and whose parents shared for a while the same aspirations with King's and moved in the same social circles, records in his *To Kill a Black Man* (Holloway House, 1968) that this was also the era during which "major newspapers began to hire Negro reporters . . . there were few white reporters, excluding those from the Deep South, who did not feel and write as we did. It is no detraction from Martin to say that but for the news media he would have remained an unsung clergyman."

Nonviolence was a tactic that was developing in Montgomery. It had been used before. Black people had paraded down Fifth Avenue to the beat of a solitary snare drum, protesting the lynching that was so widespread in the South in 1917. In the Depression years, groups of workers had employed it with some success, and during World War II, some members of the Fellowship of Reconciliation, Bayard Rustin among them, went to jail to protest their opposition to the war and the draft.

Nonviolence was the *only* tactical weapon black people had at their command. In Montgomery itself, it had been employed by E. D. Nixon, head of the Progressive Democrats, former state chairman of the National Association for the Advancement of Colored People (which had been banned in Alabama) and a member of A. Philip Randolph's Brotherhood of Sleeping Car Porters. Nixon had been pretty much running whatever movement existed in Montgomery, before King's arrival. It was Nixon who had formulated a nonviolent tactic, based on his union experiences. It was Nixon who in the first place gathered the ministers of Montgomery to protest the arrest of Mrs. Rosa Parks, proposing a one-day boycott of the city's buses. And it was Nixon's group, the Interdenominational Ministerial Alliance, that would give way to the Montgomery Improvement Association. Had Nixon been in Montgomery and not on the road at the time the officers were elected it is very likely that he, not King, would have been its president. Instead, *in absentia,* Nixon was made treasurer.

It has been said that King was elected to his post because he had fewer enemies in town than others, but it has also been said that his election was rammed through in the absence of people who would have voted otherwise. "The people who were close to the MIA then don't want to talk about that election," a black reporter told me.

But King did become the head of the organization. Almost at once he labeled the boycott an act of "noncooperation," but a fully developed program of nonviolence based on the philosophy of Satyagraha, Gandhi's philosophy, was absent in Montgomery in 1955, and Meredith correctly stated, "King's philosophy was not thought out then; all the thinking came after."

King's education and religious training had rarely touched on the philosophies of the eastern religious scholars. The works of Wieman, Tillich, Hegel, Dessoir, Kant, Lotze, and the like, are all deeply Protestant and inclusively Anglo-Saxon; there is no place among them for the contemplative eastern religious view of God. Yet, curiously, nearly all things seem to meet in the Greeks, for King's fondness for explaining *agape,* his basic belief in it, was not far afield from the philosophy of Satyagraha. King did not know that then, but the immediate comparison by the press between "noncooperation" and the Gandhian philosophy was good enough. Of course, a movement that was nonviolent in nature could not have been led by a soldier. It could only have been led by a minister, and the black minister is a traditional figure on the American scene, one white people are used to and find extremely comforting. And Martin King behaved pretty much in the way they expected him to. However, even then things were happening that would outlast him.

For example, during the year the boycott was in effect, the

black people of Montgomery became a group that operated largely without class differences—at least in the white public eye. Upper-class Negroes shared cars and gave rides to lower-class blacks. At that level there was the kind of one-class cohesion that would not be observed again among most blacks until the late 1960's. Furthermore, the boycott forecast in the South the "white backlash" that would later become national. The irony of the Montgomery situation was that the black people there did not ask for much. As King was to write in his *Stride Toward Freedom* (Harper & Row, 1958): "Even when we asked for justice within the segregation laws, 'the powers that be' were not willing to grant it."

At that point King was not aware, really, that there is no such thing as justice within segregation laws; there is an inherent contradiction, and one comes away from such a statement with the feeling that the MIA wanted "the man merely to lighten the load a little." The MIA had requested a modification of the seating arrangements on a first-come, first-seated basis, with the blacks filling up the bus from back to front and whites from the front to where the Negroes were sitting. The MIA also requested courteous treatment from the drivers and the revocation of their police powers.

In other words, the Negroes asked for what they had been getting all along, with minor modifications. The stupidity and short-sightedness of the Montgomery city officials forced the MIA to take its case to higher courts, and on November 13, 1956, the U.S. Supreme Court upheld the decision of the U.S. District Court that Alabama's state and local laws which embodied racial segregation throughout public accommodations, were unconstitutional.

So, ironically, the segregationists helped to create Martin King, the public man. Had they given in to the limited, mild requests of the MIA there might not have been this black Christian who for the next thirteen years cried for racial justice. He might have remained, for all his education, just one more black Baptist preacher in the Deep South, capable of stirring the sisters to frequent wails, capable of making the brothers rock back on their heels to study him better.

The boycott had had a deep and visible impact on Martin King. The dapper young minister, who had been known as Tweed at Morehouse, had matured during the months in Montgomery. The eight bombings had done it; the confrontations with cracker officials had done it, but the press had done most of it. At the conclusion of the boycott, King conferred with Louis Lomax and both agreed that King could never go back—never go back to being just a minister. From then on it was forward into the mainstream of the American conscience.

Recalling his meeting with King during which all the activities that had gone on in Montgomery were reviewed, Lomax writes, "What we did not realize was that certain white men and events would make the choice" for King to become as famous as he did.

The press proclaimed him, proclaimed him and acclaimed the success of nonviolence in Montgomery. A black leader had been discovered to bring his people through this time of crisis. Full-blown now came the comparisons to Ghandi, and later, King would even make a kind of pilgrimage to India. In one of his many press conferences (he kept a list of every reporter who had come to Montgomery) King observed that the tactics of nonviolent boycott might be equally useful to hasten compliance with the Supreme Court's ruling on the desegregation of schools. The press at large and its national readership seemed much taken with the sight of numerous nonviolent black people bent in prayer—a reassuring picture indeed whose effects can be measured against those of armed black students coming out of university building they have occupied or Black Panthers in a running gun battle with the Oakland, New York, Chicago, or Los Angeles police.

For King personally, Montgomery was a tremendous success. He had become his own man, no longer the son of Martin Luther King, Sr. The father had attempted to dissuade

King from continuing on in Montgomery after his home was bombed, and had enlisted the aid of men the younger King knew and respected. But King had returned to the boycott, breaking his father's hold over him.

Carried away by the triumph in Montgomery, King said, "True pacifism is not unrealistic submission to evil power as [Reinhold] Niebuhr contends. It is rather a courageous confrontation of evil by the power of love, in the fact that it is better to be the recipient of violence than the inflicter of it, since the latter only multiplies the existence of violence and bitterness in the universe, while the former may develop a sense of shame in the opponent, and thereby bringing about a transformation and a change of heart."

Congratulatory mail poured in from all over the world; nameless hundreds of thousands blessed King. The famous wished him well. His detractors cursed him and left their letters unsigned. But it was clear that the "orderly, democratic process" had been followed to the letter. King had proved, or so it seemed then, that it could be done successfully. His mail had also brought him an invitation to attend the independence celebrations in Ghana. Going to the celebrations was a man who sat next to power, Richard M. Nixon, then Vice President under Eisenhower. Adam Clayton Powell, Ralph Bunche, A. Philip Randolph, and others were aboard the same plane. Young Dr. King was in high-flying company indeed.

Three

AFTER leaving Africa where he had also visited Nigeria, King went to Europe—to Rome, Paris, London, and Geneva. In Paris he saw the expatriate black novelist Richard Wright; they spent the better part of one day talking. I find it remarkable now that neither man in his writings has mentioned the visit or what they talked about. Wright, we know, had an abiding caution about preachers that verged on total mistrust. Friends of Wright report that he said of the meeting that he thought King was an honest man.

But now the triumphal journey was over; there was business at home, new business. In the wake of the boycott the Southern Christian Leadership Conference had been formed with King at its head. It was a rather cumbersome coalition of about 100 church or church-oriented organizations. SCLC was born during the late-night conversations of Ella Baker, who became its first executive director, Bayard Rustin, and Stanley Levinson who would become SCLC's attorney and adviser and in many cases, fund-procurer.

A very special effort was to be made to avoid conflict with the NAACP. To that end, SCLC structured no membership program, which was the backbone of the NAACP's national organization. Over the ensuing years a determined effort to raise King to the status of Roy Wilkins was an undergirding activity of SCLC, and the frequent joint marches were calculated to present to the public an image of harmony between the organizations.

Although still pastor of the Dexter Avenue Baptist Church

of Montgomery, president of the Montgomery Improvement Association, and now president of the Southern Christian Leadership Conference, Martin King by now belonged to the whole of America. William Robert Miller in his biography of King notes that the young civil rights leader gave more than 200 talks during 1957.

Early that year, however, on the third anniversary of the Supreme Court's decision on desegregation to be exact, King, together with Roy Wilkins and A. Philip Randolph headed a Prayer Pilgrimage for Freedom. Bayard Rustin who had gone to Montgomery to help organize the boycott, and who would be in the wings for the thirteen years that King lived as a national figure, helped to get the program together. Ella Baker was there, too, like Rustin, always ready just offstage to rush out and lend a hand.

About 40,000 marchers showed up at the Lincoln Memorial, and late in the afternoon King delivered his "Give Us the Ballot" speech which appeared to be designed to coincide with the NAACP's voting rights drive. Wilkins' organization had put up a major share of the money for the pilgrimage.

For a year now King had been asking government officials from the President down to make a statement on the intensifying situation in the South, or to pay a visit. Only Nixon had responded, asking King to visit him, though he had not indicated that the visit was to be official. From the rest of the administration, nothing—nothing for the man who'd made the cover of *Time* magazine as the leader of the boycott. The administration appeared to be fearful that such a meeting would infuriate Southerners for one thing, and raise the question of racial disharmony to the level of national importance for another. The Eisenhower Administration, as was its habit, stuck its head in the sand and hoped that when it pulled it out the problem would have vanished.

No matter. Martin King's popularity did not depend on a White House meeting or on Eisenhower's statement that "you can't legislate men's hearts."

His life was filled with writing, speaking, and organizing. The second time he tried to go to jail in 1956, his fine was paid by a Montgomery city official—so that King couldn't use the jail "as a publicity stunt." Later, in Harlem, while autographing copies of his first book, *Stride Toward Freedom* (Harper & Row, 1958), he was stabbed by a Mrs. Izola Curry.* The wound was nearly fatal, but he survived. When he recovered, he left the states to visit India with Coretta and Dr. Lawrence Reddick, a friend and author of a book about King, *Crusader Without Violence* (Harper & Row, 1959).

While King was traveling in India, where Prime Minister Jawaharlal Nehru was speaking against the solidly entrenched caste system, I was in western Europe where nearly everyone was talking about "Leetle Rock" or "Dr. Marteen Luter Keeng."

Nineteen fifty-nine was a restless year. I think people glance at calendars more during the last year of a decade and wonder where the time has gone, wonder what, after all, was accomplished with and by it. Five years had passed since the desegregation ruling, and dents in the Southern system could hardly be noticed. Although there were hundreds of Southern cities and towns, no more than forty had desegregated their bus systems. Since the Montgomery boycott both black and white have learned—blacks to their impatience and deepening frustration, and whites to their pleasure and relief—that the American sociopolitical system is designed to, and does, absorb a greater number of minority group demands than they ever believed possible—absorb them without altering the pattern, pace, or practice of society, without altering the foundations one millimeter.

Spring came to the American South in the wake of the lynching of Mack Parker in Poplarville, Mississippi. An ex-Marine Corps man, Robert Williams, organized an armed patrol in Monroe County, North Carolina, and exchanged gun-

---

* Mrs. Curry was sent first to Bellevue Hospital's psychiatric ward, and later was committed to Matteawan State Hospital for the Criminally Insane.

fire with whites who almost nightly rode through the Negro section and shot it up.

I was covering the NAACP convention in New York that year for Radio WOV and had a chance to talk with Williams. Rob was a big, hulking bear of a man, but soft-spoken and positive about the value of meeting violence with violence. Wilkins and other officials of the organization had publicly dismissed Williams from his position as head of the Monroe County NAACP; now, attorney Conrad Lynn was defending his action before a special committee that met to consider whether Williams should remain ousted or be returned to his post. For Williams it didn't matter one way or the other; he had found a workable answer. Whites no longer came into the Negro sections to terrorize blacks. In the end Williams was relieved of his post; within the next year he was to flee to Cuba, then to China and Africa.*

The NAACP position on Williams was designed to protect its integrity and to pacify its powerful white constituency, which believed deeply in the organization's vaunted legal procedures. Taking the law into one's own hands was not the NAACP "thing." Williams had to go, for he was a threat to established go-through-the-court routine. It just happened that his ouster in the final analysis gave the NAACP the appearance of going along with King's philosophy of nonviolence. The Rob Williams incident preceded by only a few months the protect-yourself talk of the Black Muslims.

King's return, therefore, was not nearly as placid as his leaving had been. Nonviolence had been on stage for nearly five years and the nation was tense. King himself had matured in appearance. He no longer wore the wide-brimmed hats; his ties were quieter; his mustache had thickened, was no longer the shaped, pencil-thin stroke of hair. His face was fuller and his feline eyes were keener, even though shadows had begun to accumulate in them. Traveling abroad he had had no fear that some person would break from a crowd and

* Williams returned to the United States in September, 1969.

try to kill him. When he slept, he slept the sleep of the secure, without the fear that dynamite was being planted under his front porch. But now he was back in the United States of America and death dogged his every footstep. King had been pastor of Dexter for five years, five fantastic years; it was time for him to resign, to take advantage of what "history has thrust upon me."

Then almost as if he had checked the course of the past years and found mistakes in his actions, King said, "We must employ new methods of struggle involving the masses of people."

The Black Muslims had compiled an enviable record in reclaiming black people from the absolute backwashes of life; they worked in the streets, the prisons, the depths of ghettoes. Their efforts and successes (exaggerated by the press) were not lost on King. What was happening was simply the unwillingness of white America to move, and in the process, blacks were cast against blacks to see which group could come up with the solution.

The Kings moved to Atlanta; he would co-pastor his father's church but devote most of his time to SCLC. Martin, Sr. was immensely relieved at the move. He had wanted his son out of Montgomery long ago and, Bayard Rustin relates, on bended knee, had begged his son to give up the Dexter Avenue post and the MIA.

The new decade began with a rush. The activities seemed to be in the command of youth; it was the time of the sit-ins. Each escalation of the civil rights movement has a date and place. The sit-ins commenced on February 1, 1960. The place was North Carolina A & T College in Greensboro. The students were directly influenced by the Montgomery bus boycott with its nonviolent philosophy; its effectiveness persuaded the black youth that they, too, could successfully employ it.

I watched the sit-ins from a vantage point of 1,700 miles away.

Late in January, 1960, I received a call from Bayard Rustin. He asked if I would organize a rally for the National Committee for a Sane Nuclear Policy in Madison Square Garden. I agreed; it was one of the things I could do well, and the pay was attractive. I'd known Rustin since 1958 when I was information man and fund-raiser for the American Committee on Africa. Rustin was on the board of directors. I assumed that he called me because I had more or less, and sometimes less, run an affair at the Waldorf Astoria for Kwame Nkrumah when he came to the United States as head of the new nation, Ghana.

You need a roster of important people if you're going to produce a successful rally. Harry Belafonte was the most difficult "important people" to get. Through novelist John O. Killens, who'd done screenplays for Belafonte, I was invited to a meeting that Belafonte was scheduled to attend. It took place on a bitterly cold night in February in the home of Judge Hubert Delaney on West 145th Street. I had no idea what kind of meeting it was going to be; I was only there to hustle Belafonte.

Belafonte and his wife, Julie, were there; Killens, a couple of black reporters who were cautioned about the timing of their releases, Judge and Mrs. Delaney, a union man from Walter Reuther's office, and a few others. There was constant traffic back and forth to the telephone, and finally I understood that the meeting was about and in support of the sit-ins, one of which was taking place at that moment. At one point in the meeting Belafonte suggested draping the Statue of Liberty in black to signify both mourning for dead liberties and the oppression of black people. I thought it a very good idea. (Some years later, an integrated group was accused of attempting to blow up the statue altogether.) *

The sit-ins which had commenced at North Carolina A & T College in Greensboro, and attracted many students, a good

---

* Belafonte did appear at the Sane rally, along with numerous other stars and leaders, and brought the house down several times with his performance.

number of them white, spurted in every direction, like quicksilver. SCLC, CORE, and FOR were caught by surprise by the speed with which they spread and the attention they attracted. However, once FOR and CORE saw that the sit-ins were a part of their own long-range plans, they supported them with classes in nonresistance and nonviolent techniques and with money and advice.

Three months later King had caught up with the still spreading sit-ins. A Good Friday meeting had been called at Shaw University by Ella Baker, and King was to address it. Ralph Abernathy, who had succeeded King as president of the MIA, was begged to lead a sit-in at the Montgomery courthouse. He did, and it was a failure, mostly because by the time he was persuaded to lead it, most of the students had given up on him. This was indicative of how the young people, influenced by adults in the first place, had almost had to drag their elders back into the situation. The result of the grown-ups' vacillation was that the kids lost faith in them, including Martin King. The students at the Shaw meeting were but a minority of the black kids in the South. A potent minority though—one that would become the Student Nonviolent Coordinating Committee. Most of the financial support for SNCC would come from the mainly white Northern Student Movement. There was some small, initial monetary support from SCLC, but it was given grudgingly.

Miss Baker was not impressed with King's talk at the Shaw meeting, but then she had always had reservations about what he set his sights on. As he spoke, King must have been thinking of the fight he'd been having since February, the fight for his very survival as a Negro leader. He had been charged with falsely swearing to information contained in his 1956 and 1958 state income tax returns.

The New York *Herald Tribune* reported: "Dr. King was the first man ever indicted under an Alabama felony statute for falsely swearing to information contained in a state tax return."

Six weeks after the Shaw meeting King was cleared on one count for 1956. The second count was not brought up again. Judge Hubert Delaney, King's attorney, and his wife Coretta, broke down with relief. They knew how remote a chance a black man had of obtaining justice in a Southern court. Innocence or guilt was never the question; color always was. King's triumph in being cleared of the state tax charge served to increase his popularity. Again he had beaten the system.

But this was King's initial experience in the intricacies of the establishment. True, he had been bombed, hauled into court, reviled, booked, jailed, and condemned in the Southern press, but he had survived, and, in fact, thrived. The establishment has at its command more than one way to break someone it has allowed to become a public figure. This was one of the commonest methods. Later, King would run head on into the others.

He had no way of knowing he would be acquitted when he spoke at Shaw University. He missed the point of the meeting. The kids did not want preaching. They had been arrested, beaten, and gassed by the hundreds. They wanted leadership. Because of his trial he could not give it. As Miss Baker put it, "He preached rather than dealt with." Methodist Minister James M. Lawson, another speaker, was on the right track, many felt, when he suggested that nonviolence be used as a *political* weapon rather than a moral one.

Many people writing on King, among them historian Lerone Bennett, Jr., described him as a father to the youngsters at that meeting. But there is always a point at which the son, quietly, for fear of upsetting the father's eqlibrium, goes his own way, easing off in that direction an inch at a time. Some say it was at this point in time when the kids began calling King De Lawd.

Four

NINETEEN sixty was the last election year capable of stirring some excitement among black Americans. Eisenhower was on the way out. On the whole the eight-year Republican stint had been for them a period of marking time. It was true that during the Eisenhower Administration the Supreme Court had brought in the desegregation ruling, that the President had sent troops into Little Rock and overseen, more or less, the passage of the Civil Rights Acts of 1957 and 1960.

Like the Emancipation Proclamation, the words had gone out, but implementation had been sadly lacking. The words that go into the makeup of laws must be accompanied by deeds. Eisenhower, like any general or former general, had a healthy regard for the striking power of the Southern bloc and the reluctant Republicans. If Warren and his court had irritated this powerful political, economic, and social coalition in 1954, Eisenhower spent the next six years appeasing them.

During his entire eight years in office there had been only one White House Conference in which King took part along with Lester Granger, then head of the National Urban League, the venerable A. Philip Randolph, and Roy Wilkins. The President had been neither helpful nor encouraging.

But now it was time for the general to leave. He'd tapped Richard M. Nixon to succeed him, but black people did not expect much from him either. Hubert H. Humphrey, whose civil rights record at that time could withstand the most grueling examination, was pitted in the primaries against Senator John F. Kennedy. Kennedy's record was not as long, and it was often fuzzy around the edges. Nevertheless Negroes hoped for a Democratic victory; no one could be as stolid or as unmoved by the cresting tide of black frustration as the Republicans.

While the Eisenhower Administration had slighted King officially, denying him access to it and the President, the public did not. King was energetic and visible, forever on the move, speaking, explaining his philosophy, raising money for SCLC. In the Congo independence came and with it civil strife; hardly a day passed without an atrocity story in the press. Nuns were reported raped and murdered by the people of Katanga province, where Patrice Lumumba had run into difficulty keeping it from seceding. Americans saw, or thought they saw, black violence gone wild in the Congo and were secretly grateful that there was a man named Martin Luther King, Jr. on these shores, preaching out against the possibility of civil disorder.

King traveled so much in 1960 that it was said that he could tell each airport by its distinctive smell. Yet he found time to write. His first book, *Stride Toward Freedom,* had a ready-made audience of Montgomery boycott watchers. Now he was working on *Strength to Love* (Harper & Row, 1963); it would not be published for another three years. This was a more difficult book. It was not a chronicle of events as was his first. In *Strength to Love* he had to lay out his philosophy, for it had in part been discovered for him.

Bayard Rustin recounts that during the early days of the boycott when King was threatened by phone calls with bombings and the murders of members of his family, he kept a handgun under the cushion of a nearby chair in the living room. He gave up the gun when friends who were serving as bodyguards almost shot a newsboy who had rustled a bush by laying his bike against it. King later spoke of this himself:

"When I decided that, as a teacher of the philosophy of non-violence, I couldn't keep a gun, I came face to face with the question of death and I dealt with it. And from that point on, I no longer needed a gun nor have I been afraid. Ultimately, one's sense of manhood must come from within."

There can be little doubt that the more King spoke and wrote the more solid became his ideas of and for nonviolence. Lerone Bennett wrote that "Throughout 1961 and 1962, Martin Luther King, Jr., was a man in search of a mission." It seems that this was even more true of 1960, at least until October. At the Southern Christian Leadership Conference on Columbus Day the delegates who had come from thirteen states, determined to escalate nonviolent direct action. They would attack segregation "in transportation, waiting rooms, schools, voter registration" and institute an economic boycott throughout the South.

Accordingly, seventy-five black college students descended on Rich's and Davidson's department stores one week later and asked for service in the restaurants. Their actions caught the black establishment by surprise, although there had been previous attempts to sit-in. These had been thwarted by intransigent whites as well as the local black elite. This time, Martin King was invited to join the sit-in, which he reluctantly did. His presence attracted the press—a consideration the kids were well aware of. They could not know that at the end of the affair King would deliver to them a deal designed to maintain the status quo for both black and white establishments.

I remember Atlanta in 1945, early in September; I remember it being hot and uncomfortable, with a kind of heavy sullenness in the air. For, after all, another war had just ended, and Southerners seem bent on relegating black veterans back to a secondary civilian status as fast as possible, lest they start demanding what all white veterans automatically receive simply because they are white. I was not used to Atlanta, nor the South, and I had met enough stomp-down crackers in the

Pacific during the war to last me ten lifetimes. I did not trust myself in that situation, and because I had no trust I had fear, so I left Atlanta with great relief and did not return until 1963.

Atlanta had long been characterized as the most forward-looking city in the South. It is the home of Atlanta University, Morehouse College, Spelman College, Morris Brown College, and Clark College. From the doors of those institutions have poured the cream of the black middle class, scholars and leaders in all fields.

With all the black intellect at its command, with all its financial resources, with all its black population, Atlanta, Georgia, should have been the first city in the South to completely desegregate; it was not. So it was that four years after he had been instrumental in shattering segregation on the buses in Montgomery, Martin King, back home now, had to lead students into the department store his family had dealt with for years and ask if he could eat at the restaurant counter.

In 1969 I asked Morris B. Abram, then President of Brandeis University, an ex-Atlantan and a lawyer long involved in civil rights causes there, why Atlanta had not been desegregated. He said he didn't know, but that he, too, found it puzzling what with all the black potential there.

I put the same question to others who had been on the scene at that time. They were black. Many white people in Atlanta who were supposed to be pulling for the blacks vanished when it came down to the nitty-gritty. Others worked as double agents. They pretended to be working for civil rights, when in reality they worked for the establishment. Morris Abram was cited as one of those people. Abram had been a long-time friend of the King family. He is believed to have been at least partially responsible for Martin King's presence at the meeting when the sit-ins were settled—settled with the restaurants to reopen resegregated.

At this point in time nearly everyone knows that King and

the students were arrested; the charge was trespassing. Thirty-seven people including King refused to put up bail. King vowed to stay in jail for as long as it took Rich's to desegregate. Mayor Hartsfield of Atlanta then managed to get the opposing parties to agree to a two-month truce for negotiating the issue and to dropping charges against King and the youngsters. Recall now that it was October 19 when the arrests were made. What need was there really for a two-month truce? No need at all except that in two months the election for the President of the United States would be over. Neither candidate, it seems to me, could have had a man of King's stature in jail while wooing the black vote. King could swing that vote, conceivably; Nixon had known him, had had some contact with him, far more than Eisenhower. And Kennedy had met him as both men swung about the nation addressing audiences. A free Martin King was a defused Martin King.

But somebody forgot to notify DeKalb County Judge Oscar Mitchell. Learning of King's arrest in Atlanta, Mitchell promptly ordered King delivered back to DeKalb where the month before he had received a twelve-month suspended sentence for driving with an out-of-state (Alabama) license. Six days after his arrest in Atlanta King was delivered to DeKalb in handcuffs and leg chains and sentenced to four months at hard labor in the closest thing possible to a Georgia chain gang.

Judge Mitchell's original sentence seems to have been designed for the specific purpose of putting King under lock and key at the very first opportunity; had it not been the incident at Rich's, it would have been something else. Mitchell was an example of the terrible, swift justice crackers hold in reserve for black people. It was immediately obvious to the nation what was afoot.

Prisoners die on road gangs. They die from beatings, they die from malnourishment, and they die from murder. Prison deaths are the most ignominious. People tend to think, "Well, if he'd been any good, he wouldn't have been in jail in the first place." The death of Martin King in the state public works camp was imminent.

A number of important people realized it. Eisenhower's Justice Department, moving with the speed of maple syrup in a sudden freeze, examined a possible position as a friend of the court before Judge Mitchell. JD decided, no good. What *would* be of some value would be a statement from President Eisenhower. The President drafted the statement, but it was never issued.

For many this recalled the Eisenhower statements of December 26, 1944, drafted when the German breakthrough all but shattered the Allied lines in what became known as the Battle of the Bulge. In his first draft Eisenhower, the Supreme Commander, specifically asked for black troops in the grades of private and private first class to volunteer for combat duty rather than continue in rear echelon service. Under pressure Ike rewrote his statement so that it did not appear to be a naked call for help from "Ethiopia" (as Secretary Seward put it when Lincoln first considered the Emancipation Proclamation in order to free blacks not so much from slavery as from duty with the South.) In matters of race Eisenhower was consistent; he did little.

Vice President Nixon, deep into the campaign and sweating over the moderate Kennedy gains in the polls, was taking no chances of upsetting the Southerners; he remained silent. The Kennedys on the other hand smelled the chitlins cooking in the farmhouse after the West Virginia primary.

On Eisenhower's death in 1969, I. F. Stone said that Eisenhower had been the triumph of a welfare state; he was its most illustrious case.

The Kennedy candidate had come down the other end of the pike where money and personal power and the exercise of it required clearance from no one. Jack Kennedy called Coretta King and said he was "concerned." Robert Kennedy lit astride Judge Mitchell's back and stayed there until King was released on $2,000 bond. The intermediaries in the tale of the two telephone calls were Mayor Hartsfield, Harris Wofford, who later wound up in the upper levels of the Peace Corps, and Morris Abram.

Martin Luther King, Sr., told his congregation that he was now a Kennedy man; Martin, Jr., still had reservations, as if they mattered. The Kennedys had interceded in his behalf. Black people didn't really care whether King endorsed Kennedy; they would, for he, perhaps, had saved King's life. King's thunder had been lifted, and neatly. He had been used to secure the votes of the masses, and it was not important whether he liked the Kennedys or not. And they knew it.

Under Eisenhower the nation had remained intransigent and unwilling to humor any immediate and tangible gains for black people. One does not rush to test the temper of a man who had a notoriously short one in certain situations. A President who is of a military disposition automatically reflects the collective subconscious of the nation that gave him the office.

John F. Kennedy was another matter. He was tough, his family was tough, and independent. It was this toughness, this independence that gave Jack Kennedy his soul-brother-like *savoir faire*. He liked a good time. Delightful rumors about him (and Robert) cracked up the cats in the pool hall as well as Negroes striving to obtain or hold onto some kind of middle class status. Kennedy's sense of humor was infectious. Today, in the light of the terrible events in the lives of the Kennedys, it almost seems as though, at some point, one Kennedy sold his soul to the devil. For tragedy has stalked this family along the road down which it came smiling brightly, easily carrying its latter-day Ivy League banners, until it is almost a family no longer. And black people say that Mrs. John F. Kennedy married Aristotle Onassis simply because she could no longer stand Americans.

But at that hopeful moment when Kennedy won the very close election, Negroes understood the New Frontier to mean a new time in American history when, at last, they would get theirs.

It was CORE and James Farmer, not King and SCLC, that moved on the spanking new Kennedy Administration with the speed of an aging quarterback throwing a pass into the territory of a rookie cornerback. King, however, agreed to serve as chairman of the Freedom Ride Coordinating Committee; SNCC also was involved, but the plan to "put the sit-ins on the road" belonged to CORE.

Various laws abolishing segregation in interstate travel had been passed for years without notable effect, the most recent being a U.S. Supreme Court ruling in December, 1960. The main reason for this was that the transportation companies, the trains and buses, refused to comply for fear they would anger their Southern affiliates.

I can remember riding Jim Crow trains. I can remember how railroad conductors in Chicago and Los Angeles and Washington always seated black people in the Jim Crow car sections, even in those "Northern" cities. With what practiced motions did the conductors wave whites rearward and blacks forward; with what meekness did we move forward, faces set in false smiles as we hurried to get a window seat through which one of those cracker kids with a .22 might fire, just for target practice. And after the degrading ride there was always at the stop or change point the station with its two water fountains, two bathrooms, one White and one Colored.

The basic aim of the sit-ins was to embarrass the nation, spur it into action to abolish the systems that ensured a life of degradation for the majority of its nonwhite citizens. The Freedom Rides were perfectly timed; surely the New Frontier offered black people freedom of interstate travel and accommodations. Nothing is quite so humiliating, so murderously angering as to know that because you are black you may have to walk a half mile farther than whites just to urinate; that because you are black you have to receive your food through a window in the back of a restaurant or sit in a garbage-littered yard to eat. So in a letter dated April 28, 1961, Farmer wrote President Kennedy informing him of the Freedom Ride itinerary and the plan to test the public accommodations at each stop. Black riders would test white facilities, and white riders would test black counters and rest rooms.

Surely it would have been a waste of time to send such a letter to the Eisenhower Administration.

May 4, 1961. Washington, D.C. Twelve Freedom Riders, intelligent people who knew they could not count on the law, much less the lawmen along their route, boarded Trailways and Greyhound buses with interstate points of call. The first two buses caught "natural hell." The riders were committed to King's nonviolent approach; they were to love the people who were trying to kill them. Forewarned that the blacks and whites were coming nonviolently, the crackers—men and women— were out in full force waiting.

The route wound South: Charlotte, North Carolina; Rock Hill, South Carolina; Winnsboro, South Carolina; Anniston, Alabama; Montgomery, Alabama; Birmingham, Alabama— wherever they went, they were met by crackers who knew the riders would not fight back. The crackers came in the grip of their white sickness, as eager to hurt and maim those who had chosen to be defenseless, as the syphilis-ridden sailors of Elizabethan England had been to go to Africa to enslave—after they raped every black girl and woman they could put their pox-polluted phalluses to.

After two weeks of travels, beatings, and humiliations—with more youngsters from Fisk University climbing aboard new buses every day to take up the slack—the denouement came in King's old stamping ground, Montgomery, Alabama. A group of Freedom Riders, Martin King, a mob of crackers, and 400 U.S. marshals sent by Robert Kennedy, converged on the city. King addressed the riders and some 1,200 supporters in the First Baptist Church that evening—a church surrounded by stomp-down crackers. Outside, a small squad of marshals and a handful of unwilling city policemen separated the Christians from the lions. Governor John Patterson declared that the U.S. marshals were unnecessary, but found himself unable to control his citizens.

Injunctions were coming out of the Federal District Court like bullets, hoping to stop the Klan from getting involved. Another 226 marshals were on the way to Montgomery; they would arrive the next morning.

As King spoke, the white mob outside shouted and threw stones into the church, smashing the windows. Faintly, into the church, seeped the odor of the tear gas the marshals were using to hold the crackers in check. No one in church knew exactly when it would be safe to leave. Up in Washington, pressure was being brought directly to bear on Governor Patterson to use the National Guard to disperse the mob. Robert Kennedy won. But even as Patterson called out the guard, he told Kennedy that Major General Henry Graham, the commander of the guard, was unable to see to the safety of Martin King. Then Robert Kennedy—so closely involved with King from 1960 until eight years later when short weeks after King was murdered, he met his own death—made a statement that revealed the best in the Kennedys: "Have the general call me. I want him to say it to me. I want to hear a general of the U.S. Army say he can't protect Martin Luther King, Jr."

Patterson boogalooed on one foot; he admitted that he, not the general, believed nothing could save King from the mob.

King and the people were saved, and the Freedom Rides continued. A bus was leaving for Jackson, Mississippi, the following morning at seven, carrying riders, reporters, and armed soldiers. Lerone Bennett reports that there were also twenty-two highway patrol squad cars, three planes and two helicopters for reconnaissance and two battalions of national guardsmen. With mixed emotions, King watched the mighty entourage leave Montgomery. The strength of the government had been employed finally. But that power could better have been used earlier, to effect implementation of the law.

I rarely travel by bus, except to and from airports, but when I do I always note the crisp sign that reads: SEATING ABOARD THIS VEHICLE WITHOUT REGARD TO RACE, COLOR, CREED, OR NA-

TIONAL ORIGIN, BY ORDER OF THE INTERSTATE COMMERCE COM-
MISSION. And I wonder if the other passengers aboard are
aware that that simple sign was the result of beatings, shattered
teeth, broken limbs, burned buses, a massive effort on the part
of the Justice Department—not the Interstate Commerce Commission—and as ugly a blot on the American way of life as
had been witnessed since Little Rock.

However, if one is convinced as I am that love, that nonviolence can't work *today* in the United States, it comes as no
surprise that a white mob was prepared to annihilate black and
white people within the confines of a church. Even in the
Middle Ages a serf was considered to be in sanctuary if he
could only make it through the doors of a church—not so in
America. For black people and for the whites who side with
them no sanctuary is offered.

In mid-1969 the National Commission on the Causes and
Prevention of Violence released a massive document, some
350,000 words on *Violence in America—Historical and Com-
parative Perspective.* Nonviolence, in the report, turned out
to be alien to national concepts of how to get things done.
If, then, the Freedom Riders had made their journeys, if not
armed, at least willing to trade blow for blow, there would
have been damned few mobs at those bus stations.

And Martin King knew this. As he watched, his nonviolent
philosophy was being wiped out before his eyes. The violence
that assailed the Freedom Riders, assailed him and the congregation of the First Baptist Church in Montgomery, was de-
terred only by the show of even greater violence on the part
of the government. The use of violence, King had contended,
gave the opposite party the excuse to escalate the degree of
violence until it was in his favor. So the ominous spiral went
on around him. He may have been unhappy about it, but he
had to admit to himself that violence, at least in Montgomery
that night, had prevented the possible massacre of 1,200
people.

Five

"THEY [SCLC and Martin King] went into Albany. Now, why did they go into Albany?"

The question was asked on a muggy day early in spring, 1969; it was asked by Ella Baker. The sounds of the Harlem streets—cars, children's screams, horns—speared upward to be captured on the tape along with Miss Baker's precise enunciation.

The interviewer answered her question: "Because the kids [SNCC] were already there."

"That's right," Miss Baker said.

Two SNCC people, Cordell Reagan and Charles Sherrod, had gone to Albany in November, 1961, to initiate not only voter registration but overall political participation by the blacks. In most Southern states, because votes are counted by county units, power resides in the rural rather than the urban centers; SNCC went to the heart of the power base in order to change it. Most of the black establishment was opposed to SNCC activities. It goes without saying that the white establishment was even more reticent. It is generally written that SNCC worked with the ministers there, but, in fact, their strongest opposition came from the black ministers. And the local NAACP, according to former SNCC officials. Thanksgiving week three SNCC people tried to integrate the restaurant of the bus station; fifteen days later Freedom Riders from Atlanta arrived. Wholesale arrests were made. More students joined the protest and more went to jail.

Meanwhile, back in Atlanta, Martin King and Ralph Abernathy, who had joined him at SCLC, sat in their offices, awaiting some kind of summons to go to Albany. Police chief Laurie Pritchett tried to clear the Albany streets with what he called peaceful arrests.

On the fourteenth of December the police released the 118 juvenile prisoners, and Mayor Kelley brought together a group of whites and blacks. Nothing came of the meeting, however, and Kelley stacked up a unit of the Georgia National Guard in the local armory—just in case. At this point, one of the Albany Movement leaders, Dr. William G. Anderson, called on King; on the following evening, King and the man who had been at his side in Montgomery and who would be there until he died, Ralph Abernathy, arrived in Albany and appeared at the rally.

Now here stories fall apart. Some say King was invited to lead demonstrators in protest the next day; others claim that there had been no place on the program for King, that he got to Albany when all was already in motion and simply stationed himself at the head of the nonviolent protests. In any case, King and Abernathy were arrested along with Dr. Anderson and 250 others. Mayor Kelley resumed negotiations, and the city commission agreed to desegregate bus and train terminals and to hire "at least one Negro bus driver."

The Albany actions lasted almost a year. Chief Pritchett kept the demonstrators off balance by meeting nonviolence with nonviolence. Martin King was jailed four times; four Negro churches were destroyed by crackers, although they did rebuild one of them with what Miller describes as "paternalistic zeal."

"Prayer pilgrims," clergymen and laymen, caught trains and planes to Albany, seeking to focus the shifting eyes of the nation on the problems there. Some of these people would follow King in the years to come to St. Augustine, to Birmingham, to Selma, to Washington. For many of them Albany was their first visit to a strange region in the United States, a region of fear and uncertainty, of possible injury—the region where black people have always lived. But they came and were promptly jailed when they marched in front of the Albany city hall. Most accepted bail and returned home; some fasted, a few stayed in the city jail for a week.

One powerful minister, leader of 6.5 million churchgoers, turned his back on Albany and Martin King. He was Dr. Joseph H. Jackson of the National Baptist Convention who from King's beginning had vigorously opposed "civil disobedience" and supported "law and order." * The National Baptist Convention was in session while "pilgrims" were going to Albany. Jackson turned deaf ears on all propositions to aid King. Dr. Jackson was black.

Money problems as well cropped up in Albany for SCLC. The August 18 edition of the New York *Times* for 1962 reported that SCLC activities had cost the organization about $10,000 in the previous month alone. King, Abernathy and Wyatt Tee Walker, who had joined the group, could not leave town to recoup their losses by keeping speaking engagements because they were either in jail or needed in Albany to help keep the lid on.

Also, the differences between SNCC and SCLC flared anew. "We do all the work," the SNCC people said, "and Martin King gets all the credit."

Their differences were mild when compared with another. For Albany was also the birthplace of the awkward relationship between SCLC and the Federal Bureau of Investigation whose agents were there trying both to discover who had set fire to the churches and to take complaints of brutality charged against the local police by marchers. Not long afterward King would make a statement on his assessment of the FBI in the South—a statement that would be one of the things that would

* In 1960, Dr. Jackson beat off an attempt by King and other civil-rights-oriented ministers to oust him from his office of President of the NBC. The following year Jackson discharged King from his post as vice president in charge of the youth division. Still later, Jackson replaced King as President Johnson's Negro preacher in residence.

lead him into a portentous confrontation with its director, J. Edgar Hoover.

Things were happening outside Albany in 1962 that would involve Martin King; they would build his image which had already been heightened by his participation in the Albany Movement. The first occurred in Birmingham—"Bombingham," as some blacks called it. Fred Shuttlesworth, a minister and head of the Alabama Christian Movement for Human Rights—an organization that had come into being when the NAACP was banned by the state courts—called in the spring for SCLC, of which his organization was an affiliate, to begin a nonviolent campaign in Birmingham.

The second was the violent admission of a young man named James Meredith to the University of Mississippi in June. At that time the loving Martin King's getting together with the spooky Meredith appeared highly unlikely. Upon closer examination, however, it was probably inevitable that they would cooperate in at least one venture. They did, in 1966.

But the first thing first: Birmingham.

What went on in Birmingham in spring, 1963, has been studied, analyzed, written about, and replayed again and again. We think of Birmingham then and the pictures taken during the demonstrations leap sharply back into focus in our minds: three cops, one with his knee in her neck, astride a black woman who struggles on her back, her earrings still in place, her hair freshly done and sparkling in the sun and dust; those black, determined hordes pouring down the stone steps of the Sixteenth Street Baptist Church, to fan out in all directions and bring the challenge to Safety Commissioner Eugene "Bull" Connor, among them, children.

The children. "Suffer little children to come unto me and forbid them not," et cetera, et cetera. King had used children in his marches tentatively in Albany; in Birmingham they were all over the place. The black schools were empty.

Across the nation a cry went up: "How dare he use children!

How low can King sink?" This question from the descendants of those who'd in Europe dispatched hundreds of thousands of children on a foolhardy crusade to the Holy Land. Their ranks decimated by hunger, murder, kidnapping—their doomed youngsters barely got out of the Europe that had sent them in the first place. This question from a people who barely half a century ago thought nothing of working youngsters fourteen hours a day in the nation's mills; this question from those who, in some sections of the country, had established school systems around the work hours of the young. Finally, this question from those whose forefathers had stolen black children from Africa and on these shores took them from their mothers' arms to sell.

It was almost as if the people who protested against the use of the children had come face to face with their own pasts in which children had counted for nothing.

So the children were arrested along with the adults. The Fairgrounds were used to house the prisoners, some seven years old. We remember the picture of those kids and we might also consider that the seven year olds are now thirteen and thoroughly indoctrinated in the white man's ways.

Most of all we recall the well-fed police dogs caught in mid-air by the camera's lens, caught inches away from the bodies of black teen-agers, as policemen wearing sunglasses stood wide-legged at the end of the leashes. And who has forgotten the black youngsters, as if in a rain dance, being swept back, their arms outstretched, their legs braced against the wet grasses of Kelly Ingram Park, and the firemen whose high-pressure hoses were trained on them?

Negotiations to meet the demands of SCLC and Shuttlesworth's Alabama Christian Movement for Human Rights were begun and halted; Bull Connor was blamed for intimidating the local businessmen. The state police were called in. President Kennedy federalized the Alabama National Guard and dispatched troops with riot training to two nearby bases. But this was already the second half of the battle, the half that had accomplished what the leaders of the demonstrations wished: national attention and governmental action and support.

But it had come at a terrible cost. Shuttlesworth had been injured and hospitalized * and therefore was not readily able to discern what King's moves were or were going to be. The crackers struck back with bombs, killing four little black girls and wounding twenty others while they were attending a Sunday school class in the Sixteenth Street Baptist Church.

At their memorial services, King eloquently denied that nonviolence was dead. But it remained clear to many that Birmingham had been the turning point. No longer would nonviolence remain the supreme, unquestioned philosophy or policy for black people seeking a share of America. There had been many reports of King's travels through the city's black pool halls, requesting the inhabitants to hand over their knives and handguns, to believe in nonviolence. These were the masses that the churches had not reached; these were the people, moored in the grim reality of their condition and color, who were equally cynical about white machinations and black leadership. God did not move them and surely, Martin Luther King, Jr., could not.

Perhaps most important for King when he was jailed with Abernathy in Birmingham, was his realization that the white church in America could not be counted on for support of his nonviolent philosophy. In his famous *Letter From Birmingham Jail,* a document that was prompted by a statement issued by eight Birmingham clergymen who were opposed to the Birmingham Movement and its timing, King replied in part:

"Let me take note of my other major disappointments. I have been so greatly disappointed with the white church and its leadership. Of course, there are some notable exceptions. . . .

". . . When I was suddenly catapulted into the leadership of the bus protest in Montgomery, Alabama, a few years ago, I felt we would be supported by the white church. I felt that

* Shuttlesworth had been knocked down by water from the hoses.

the white ministers, priests and rabbis of the South would be among our strongest allies. Instead, some have been outright opponents, refusing to understand the freedom movement and misrepresenting its leaders; all too many others have been more cautious than courageous and have remained silent behind the anesthetizing security of stained-glass windows."

King also assailed the "moderates" for failing to see that the "South, the nation and the world [were] in dire need of creative extremists."

At about the same time that James Meredith was finishing his first year at the University of Mississippi, Birmingham was grinding to a conclusion. On May 20 the U.S. Supreme Court struck down the city's segregation ordinances. But all the action in Birmingham seemed wasted when, in September, the crackers struck back and killed the little girls.

Between May and September, however, other items crowded King's busy agenda. June. Flushed with what appeared to be a massive triumph in Birmingham, King stepped out on a nationwide tour, but this was the same June that Medgar Evers was shot in the back and killed in Jackson, Mississippi, by Byron De La Beckwith. As King traveled to Los Angeles, Chicago, Detroit, and other cities to be hailed by the liberal white and middle-class black elements, the cattle-prod was being introduced and used throughout the South and Southeast. And in Harlem, King's car was bombarded with eggs by young blacks.

Six

YOU still hear people talking about the March on Washington, which was held on August 28, 1963. White people warmly reflect on it as a shining example of the "old days," when there was not so much caution between blacks and liberals. Black people generally remark that they knew "it wouldn't do any good"—an indication that at heart they wished it had.

As I see the March on Washington now, despite its "failure" and it *did* fail to achieve the *intangible* goals that should have been tangible—it certainly could have been a more precious moment in American history than it has become. Months after the March I returned to Washington and toured its route and the grounds over which so many people spilled, and I felt compelled to write:

> The grounds were still and cold, sterile, and it was hard to visualize once more the multitudes of people who had gathered there as barons of the American spirit to petition King John on the banks of the Runnymede, petitioning not for a new Magna Charta of guaranteed rights, but for the institution of the old.

In July I was pursuing Bayard Rustin who I heard was going to oversee the march. Rustin is one of the most difficult men in the world to reach by phone, but I endured and finally got him. I wanted to volunteer my services in the premarch plans, and he accepted them.

The march office was not far from Harlem Square, a few

steps off Seventh Avenue in a building that adjoined Friendship Baptist Church. I was assigned to work with Seymour Posner, who was then the public relations man for the New York Urban League.* I'd known Sy for about two years. My assignments were so vague as to be ridiculous. Posner didn't seem to have much work for me, and what there was he wished to do himself. Then directions weren't coming from Rustin in the downstairs office, and Posner would hardly move without them. It did little good to complain because no one listened. I found that Posner wanted to use me as an example of the "kind of people" who were volunteering time, effort, and skill to the march. Finally, after almost ten days of journeying from Lafayette Street in lower Manhattan up to Harlem to sit in a sweltering top-floor cubbyhole, I gave it up.

Even civil rights organizations have their hierarchy, their "in groups" and special hands. I do not and did not have any special contacts with such organizations. I recall that once the late Arthur Spingarn, Jr., while a president of the NAACP, became impressed with me and suggested that I contact Roy Wilkins or Henry Lee Moon to work in publicity for that organization. (I had done publicity work both in New York and Los Angeles.) But after I got in touch with the organization, weeks and months went by. I told Spingarn that I hadn't heard from them, and he specifically requested that they give me an interview, which they did, but it came to nothing.

The point here is that one must be something of a "club member," with the right kind of views, background, and aspiration, to become a member of any group. I don't mean to carp. It isn't much fun to spend July or August in New York City, in any case, and I was rather glad my obligation to the "cause" had been shunted aside. I hastily headed for East Hampton to lie in the grass and swim, planning however, to attend the march.

The words that follow are mine, but they reflect for me the spirit of the march so many, many years ago (it now seems).

* He is now a New York State assemblyman.

I have read and reread them, and concluded that I would utilize them here, for they speak of a personal mood and, in part, of the mood of the marchers. They also speak of Martin King:

I had left New York, a passenger in one of two cars filled with black people and white people. Our lunches were packed and sleep had been set aside. When we emerged from the Holland Tunnel and gained the New Jersey Turnpike, hundreds of cars and buses, like ourselves, were hurtling southward, signs snapping in the midnight wind, FREEDOM, or FREEDOM NOW. When we pulled into a Howard Johnson's later, we knew everyone in the parking lot was going to Washington. There were signs on the cars and buses, and stacks of lunches. Greetings rolled into the night and black hands and white hands together slammed car doors and proceeded on to the capital, some cars filled with waking and crying babies.

The great caravan sped on. We waved as we passed other cars and the people in them waved to us. Snatches of song were strung along the highway. On they came, the cars and buses. Sleep was impossible. The spirit soared at the sight of so many people, and the spine itched with knowing in some ancient, instinctive way that something great and electric was moving at last in the nation. By dawn the buses were already prowling toward their appointed places in the city. The cars were from everywhere, north, south and west. By ten the folk singers were at work. Their voices drifted down from the speakers set high atop the Washington Monument, now gleaming like a golden bar in the sunlight. Contingents hoisted their signs for everyone to see. Newsmen dashed through the crowds or mounted platforms. Still they came. There were more folk singers, and planes bringing more marchers droned overhead. How many thousands? The people swept from the Mall up to the foot of the shaft, 25,000; 50,000; 100,000. They were everywhere. Odetta sang, Joan Baez, the Chad Mitchell Trio. From all sides they came; they disembarked from their buses and walked down Constitution Avenue, banners and posters held high; from the airport and train stations they came. One man skated in. Finally they spilled over the mound and down over the Mall, a slowly spreading river.

And suddenly it was time to march, and over a quarter of a million people, black and white, moved down the roads to the Lincoln Memorial. They were so tightly massed that it was impossible to cross between the ranks. Overhead on lifts and mottled with the shadows of millions of leaves from the great trees that lined the streets, the television cameras swung back and forth, peered down into the crowds. The armies shuffled along singing, arm in arm, hand in hand, strangers no more, and it hurt to look into some of the faces: so close, the power of the sun at full shine. Some of the marchers were so old they had to be wheeled, and some were so young they had to be carried, and some so sightless they had to be led. Some people wept as they moved along, and unable to extricate their hands from those of their newfound friends, let the tears roll freely. Some people smiled, but they all moved with the innate grace of those endowed with a powerful purpose. The marchers pinched in from two roads, spilled onto the Mall, back, back, back, until the grass around the Reflection Pool was entirely covered with humanity. And still they came.

I sat on the steps of the Lincoln Memorial with Bob Johnson [now executive editor] of Jet, and Dick Gregory. We weren't supposed to have liquor [it was banned that day in Washington], but we had and liberally spiced our Cokes with it. ... On raised platforms before us the NBC and CBS teams with ear-phoned spotters, stood with their jackets blowing in the soft, August wind. When a group of Congressmen came in during the middle of a prayer and stopped with heads bowed, Roger Mudd of CBS leaned forward with pencil and paper. Marvin Kalb, also of CBS, paced through the crowd gathering Lena Horne, Rev. Fred Shuttlesworth and Sammy Davis for interviews.

When the prayer was over and the people spotted their representatives, like the wind leaping up far out on a plain came the chant, "Pass the bill! Pass the bill!" [King and others had been pushing for additional civil rights legislation. Despite the march, the bill would not be passed until 1964 as the Civil Rights Act of 1964.] As it moved through the ranks, the chant gained strength. "Pass the bill!" "Pass the bill!" With a sudden, almost embarrassed sigh, it faded and the program continued.

When Martin Luther King, Jr., came up to speak, the quarter million were at a fever pitch.

"I have a dream!" M. L. said.

"Tell 'em Martin!" Bob shouted. [He had been a classmate of King's at Morehouse.]

"I have a dream!" M. L. said again, and behind us, his voice lost to all but those close to him, a man screamed, "Fuck that dream, Martin! Now, goddamit, NOW!" *

The Reverend Dr. Martin Luther King, Jr.—M. L. to those who knew him in Atlanta—was scheduled to be and was the star of the march. Without him there would have been no march. The other leaders were as iron dust to King's magnet.

They represented the whole gamut of the civil rights movement: Whitney Young, Jr., National Urban League; King, SCLC; John Lewis, SNCC; Rabbi Joachim Prinz, American Jewish Congress; Reverend Dr. Eugene Carson Blake, United Presbyterian Church; A. Philip Randolph, Negro American Labor Council; Walter P. Reuther, United Auto Workers; Roy Wilkins, NAACP; Floyd McKissick, CORE (who filled in for James Farmer, the head of CORE, who was in jail in Louisiana); and Mathew Ahmann, National Catholic Conference for Interracial Justice.

But it was Martin King's day. The march was a pure, unfettered, tasteful triumph; the *I Have a Dream* speech is history now, and the dream is dead. But that day, that day. . . .

But what of the rest of America? I thought then. I return to *This Is My Country Too* for my answer that day:

"Millions of people had seen the March on television . . . *Now* what was taking place in the minds of many Americans who saw that display of power, which represented, perhaps, millions of well-wishers who hadn't the money, the time or the courage to journey to Washington? A display of power begets a display of power. . . ."

* *This Is My Country Too.* New York, New American Library-World, 1965.

It did not have a name then, but of course I was writing about the birth of backlash. As for those millions of "well-wishers," they vanished; they zipped over the horizon to the other side when is became clear that black freedom was not merely a matter of eloquent rhetoric and good intentions—like the Emancipation that *proclaimed* freedom, but failed to guarantee it—but a matter of vital interest to the very well-being of the nation as a whole.

While the march was in the planning, while it was being carried out, nearly all was calm and in order. King's *Letter From Birmingham Jail,* chastening the churches and churchmen of America, had galvanized them into march participation. Significantly, however, the National Council of the gigantic AFL-CIO did not support the march, though member unions independently did. The American trade unions today, belying their radical liberalism of the twenties and thirties, are one of the most powerful strongholds of bigotry in existence. Perhaps they always were.

And at the other end of the economic scale, Hollywood stars appeared at the march, garnered all possible publicity—and have not been seen or heard at another civil rights rally since. (Marlon Brando remains an exception.) Forgotten was the memorial to dead Medgar Evers.

As the day drew to a close, people sauntered around as if reluctant to return to their homes. Interracial couples with their children held placards proclaiming the oneness of all peoples; a small group of American Nazis walked in a circle chanting, and the late George Lincoln Rockwell, head of the group, said in an interview that he had not asked members of the Ku Klux Klan to join him. "They are anti-Catholic. Some of our best people are Catholics."

When the marchers finally began to leave, Washingtonians who had crept out of the city the evening before, fearful of racial violence, crept back in while the soldiers who had been strategically stationed and hidden in groves of trees around the memorial and in various government buildings, assembled their gear and prepared to depart.

March leaders gathered in the White House with President Kennedy who in a prepared statement ironically linked the aspirations of the march to a salute to labor and Labor Day. Like so many others, he applauded the leaders and marchers for having demonstrated peaceably. Peaceably, peacefully, quietly, orderly—those were the descriptions given the march. It was plain that many had believed the march would turn into the rebellions that erupted in 1965 in Watts. In psychological terms, a man *should* expect violence if he knows he has wronged another.

Martin King was not unaware of the potential for violence. The fact that it did not occur, that he was the stopper for black violence, made him the nation's undisputed "Negro Leader." The *Newsweek* poll of July, 1963, anticipated this; its second poll, in October of the same year, confirmed it. The Southern Christian Leadership Conference was all but lost in the shuffle; SCLC was Martin King.

At the absolute peak of his career in October, 1963, according to William Brink and Louis Harris, the *Newsweek* pollsters, King returned once again to the campaign in Atlanta to nibble at segregation in his own home town. While King was thus engaged, I took to the road on a long trip to see what the nation was like, thinking *that* was a time of racial crisis!

During those travels, north and south, east and west, I stopped for a while in Atlanta, where there was some bitterness about King's prominence; many felt he had deserted the local battle for national acclaim. A young man connected with Operation Breadbasket, an SCLC program devised in 1962 to bring pressure on local businesses in a number of cities to employ blacks, told me that there was a move afoot to find a local leader to replace King. Others were not so critical, but then nearly all of them had grown up with King.

The nation thought itself in turmoil in 1963, though; that was clear as I traveled around the country. But it hadn't seen anything yet. In Detroit black activists were protesting that city's invitation to the International Olympic Committee to hold the games there in 1968. San Francisco was already locked in a close mayoral election between Harold Dobbs and John F. Shelley with racial overtones—a preview of what would sweep other American cities in years to come.

In November, heroic, democratic, Christian good-people-down-deep Americans killed their fourth President, John F. Kennedy.

While King had never let up on him, criticizing his administration and Kennedy's own lacks in the civil rights battles, he said in *Why We Can't Wait* (Harper & Row, 1964) "And yet, had President Kennedy lived, I would probably have endorsed him in the forthcoming election."

Of the Kennedy murder King said in the same book, "Negroes know political assassination well. In the life of Negro civil-rights leaders, the whine of the bullet from ambush, the roar of the bomb have all too often broken the night's silence. They have replaced lynching as a political weapon. . . . Nineteen sixty-three was a year of assassinations. Medgar Evers in Jackson, Mississippi; William Moore in Alabama; four Negro children in Birmingham—and who could doubt that these too were political assassinations?"

I wondered if King allowed the reality of his own existence to take over his thoughts as he wrote those words. Words merely describe reality, they are in fact not it. But perhaps King was one of the new breed who discovers that talking and writing about death often have the facility of making one ready to meet it. Did King seek death? Did he, once he was on the treadmill of fame and leadership, refuse to get off because he saw, even embraced, his end?

James Meredith believes King wished to die. Other people I interviewed, whatever else they believed about King, were certain of his willingness to die for the cause of nonviolent change. As a youngster King had twice hurled himself from the second floor of his home and both times escaped unhurt. But the death wish of a youngster is far different from the death wish of an adult; the longer one lives, the more fiercely one tends to grip life. Or so it is with most people.

The documents of the slave trade show that much of the harsh treatment accorded the slaves during the Middle Passage—the chains, the bolting to the decks—was because the slaves showed an alarming (to the slavers) willingness to commit suicide rather than endure slavery. Once on these shores, however, the will to live took over, and perhaps the deepest emotion then was one of revenge on whites for what they had done. In order to secure revenge, though, one must, in most cases, possess life. Now it appears that there are enough lives and enough learning about white American society and the will and wish and commitment to change or destroy it, even if it means death.

Nineteen sixty-three drew to a close with Lyndon Johnson trying to pick up the shattered fragments of the Kennedy administration and pull the country together; King, again in *Why We Can't Wait*, expressed cautious optimism about the new President's programs: "... the dimensions of Johnson's leadership have spread from a region to a nation. His recent expressions, public and private, indicate that he has a comprehensive grasp of contemporary problems. He has seen that poverty and unemployment are grave and growing catastrophes, and he is aware that those caught most fiercely in the grip of this economic holocaust are Negroes. Therefore, he has set the twin goal of a battle against discrimination within the war on poverty."

I finished my four-and-a-half month trip around the nation, finding both the usual American bigotry and new friends, black and white. Then I left the country for Europe, the Middle East, and Africa, where there was sadness and horror over Kennedy's murder and something like hope for America because Martin King was still alive and well.

Seven

NINETEEN sixty-four was a year of tremendous importance to the young people of this nation who were (and still are) looking for a cause, a place to pour their energies and strengths. Not all were interested in the Peace Corps; many saw their obligations at home. The COFO Summer, as it has been called, gave many the opportunity for the first time to see just how rotten their nation was. COFO—Council of Federated Organizations—was composed of SCLC, CORE, NAACP, and SNCC, and local groups and union locals. Books and college students went southward in groups. The students had been given an orientation program in the customs of the South, in nonviolence, in Oxford, Ohio. Their goal was to organize, to press blacks to register to vote. SNCC watched all the enthusiasm with great detachment; they had already lived with rural blacks; they had been hounded by the local police, the cracker drugstore cowboys. They knew there was a tremendous job ahead and were glad for the help. That was March; by the end of June those kids from the North, black and white, would come to know the guts of America. Years afterward when someone would mention Philadelphia, they would think of Philadelphia, *Mississippi,* not Pennsylvania.

King had begun 1964 as *Time* Magazine's Man of the Year for 1963; he had been called Symbol of the Revolution, in that centennial year of the Emancipation Proclamation. Haile Selassie had been the first black man on the *Time* cover, in 1927. King was the second. There was no doubt in the minds of millions that King was supposed to live up to all *Time* said about him. And not only King, who was "the representative of his people," but the people, those masses of middle-class blacks who sought peaceful, nonviolent solutions to their condition.

Writing, speaking, and traveling, King eased into 1964 headlines in the oldest city in the United States—St. Augustine, Florida. St. Augustine was a city where many Americans went to tour the historic sites—including the old slave market. Writer Paul Good observed in St. Augustine that "Where Negroes once could not walk freely out [of the slave market] in 1964 they could not walk freely in" for their demonstrations.

Dr. R. N. Hayling, a dentist, was the local NAACP leader in St. Augustine and had encouraged the young people in their sit-ins in 1961, with disastrous results to them at the hands of the Klan. At will the Klan kidnapped blacks and shotgunned their homes. In March of 1964 King and Hayling agreed that King was needed in St. Augustine. The campaign there got under way while King was busy in Alabama, trying to force an advantageous confrontation with George Wallace.

As is well known now, on Easter Sunday an interracial group of women, among them Mrs. John Burgess whose husband was the first black bishop in the Episcopal church, and Mrs. Malcolm Peabody, the mother of Governor Endicott "Chub" Peabody of Massachusetts, attempted to take communion at St. Augustine's Trinity Episcopal Church; they were refused entrance and were arrested. Mrs. Peabody was seventy-two years old.

Tension mounted between Easter Sunday and May when King arrived. The local sheriff forbade further night marches to the old slave market, claiming that he could not protect the marchers; indeed, it was clear that he had no desire to. Police chief Virgil Stuart backed up his decision, telling the Reverend Andy Young, a King assistant, that the marchers would be hurt as never before, if the marches continued through the Klansmen.

Stuart's police force was composed of eighteen men; when the marches were scheduled they were nowhere to be found. But SCLC went to the U.S. district court, and early in June the court found in the SCLC's favor and issued an injunction forbidding Sheriff Davis and Chief Stuart from stopping the marches. Of course, the order had no effect; marchers were still beaten. In the meantime, King and Abernathy tried to secure service in the Monson Motor Lodge; it was refused them, and they were arrested and confined for two days in the county jail.

Even as the campaign in St. Augustine was being conducted, Congressional leaders and President Johnson were readying the Civil Rights Act of 1964 for signature. Compliance was slow to come to St. Augustine. And at the same time over in Mississippi, there appeared to be another case of murderous defiance on the part of the crackers; James Chaney, Andrew Goodman, and Michael Schwerner, COFO workers, were missing. They were still missing on July 2, when King went to Washington for the signing of the bill.

Two months earlier, Ella Baker, at the behest of SNCC with which she now worked, went to Washington from Mississippi to help set up the offices of the Mississippi Freedom Democratic Party. She had prevailed on Martin King to do a whirlwind tour of Mississippi to drum up support for MFDP by visiting the voter registration centers. King stumped for five days, from June 20 to June 24. When he returned to Washington, he learned of the missing COFO workers, Chaney, Goodman, and Schwerner. Like millions of other people, he hoped against hope that they would be found alive.

Ella Baker held that hope, too, but her work with MFDP kept her busy. The organization was raising the most basic questions by its very formation and presence. It was widely known that the Southern states forbade the registration and voting of blacks in nine-tenths of cases. Therefore, no Southern Congressman, no Southern delegation to the national conventions, was truly representative of the people. It had been that way for 100 years. Even in towns and villages where blacks outnumbered whites, there was no black representation.

I had met some MFDP people while traveling through Mississippi in 1963. They were busy forging the first mixed ticket in the state since Reconstruction. Aaron Henry, a black pharmacist, was running for governor, while the Reverend Edwin King, a white, was candidate for lieutenant governor. I tried to talk with Edwin King and others on the campus of Tougaloo Southern Christian College, but our conversation was interrupted because he had to go bail out his campaign workers; they were harassed every day by the police and jailed on the flimsiest excuses. But they had managed to put their thing together by summer, 1964. They were now in a position to challenge the regular Mississippi delegation to the Democratic Convention in Atlantic City.

Early in August, while MFDP was preparing to mount its challenge, the bodies of Chaney, Goodman, and Schwerner were discovered. Many suspected then, even before it was proved, that the local police were involved in the murders. These were the same police who, two years later, would menace King and the people who joined him in Philadelphia to memorialize their deaths. When the bodies were discovered, a lot of kids realized that though they had not gone South to die, still death stalked the countryside. A chilling fear swept the ranks of the young, black and white, who had kept at arms length the terrible truth of Dixie. Parents deluged their children with telegrams urging them to quit and return home; some did, but most stayed.

Briefly, and with its usual insincere excesses, the nation, at first shocked, or apparently so, mourned with Schwerner's wife, Rita, the Goodman parents, and James Chaney's mother, but the poet-playwright-activist Le Roi Jones noted in a Greenwich Village cafe that even in death the degree of their dying was different. Chaney's body had been chain-whipped and mutilated; the others were shot, too, but not as badly torn up. The murders gave the MFDP—so it thought—additional ammunition with which to solidly challenge the regular Mississippi delegation to the convention. In addition to the murders, which were being announced and analyzed by the press, a century of deliberate white terrorism at the polls was being presented to the credentials committee by MFDP members. By any *just* reasoning their challenge was justifiable.

As if MFDP did not face enough of an uphill battle, one that carried the seeds of the destruction of the modern Democratic Party, the members were being counseled by advisers who held opposing views. In the beginning all were firmly opposed to settling for anything less than the complete removal or dismissal of the regular delegation. King led MFDP in this stand. Lyndon Johnson's aides, among them Vice President Hubert Humphrey, offered up a compromise, which many of the members accepted, King among them, and tried to sway the body at large to accept it. The Democrats had offered MFDP two seats, with the promise that, at the next convention, four years hence, they would get more. King's switch soured not only the SNCC people on him again, but the representatives of the grass roots masses like Fannie Lou Hamer.

If King was upset, no one knew it, for he now boarded a plane, just as he had after the Birmingham campaign, and flew to Europe to accept an invitation that had been tendered by the then mayor of West Berlin, Willy Brandt. With him was Ralph Abernathy. In Berlin they crossed the wall without a pass and visited the sector held by the Russians. Then they flew to Rome (and an audience with the Pope) and Madrid.

King returned determined to stump for Lyndon Baines Johnson, convinced that he now had to take an active part in politics with the appalling specter of the possibility of Barry Goldwater gaining the White House. King was high on Johnson, and Johnson had indicated his reliance on King by inviting him to the White House soon after taking office on Kennedy's death. Like many black people whose homes remain in the South or with Southern roots not quite honed sharp by the pavements of the Northern black communities, King believed that a white Southern President would do more for black people than one who had been born and raised in the North.

The signs were becoming numerous that Johnson was headed for a landslide victory, and certainly the combination of King out subtly beating the hustings for him, and Goldwater's thinly veiled threats against the black community, brought the Texan a fantastically high percentage of the Negro vote. However, the 1964 election was not the only thing on King's mind, for during the year there had been persistent rumors that he was going to be nominated for the Nobel Peace Prize. The rumors were finally confirmed in October, 1964, at a time when most pollsters agreed that Barry Goldwater was going to be thoroughly wasted by Johnson. Most Negroes were happy about that, but a friend of mine who was deeply involved with the administration later, remarked, "Nigger is a household word in Johnson's White House. You hear it all the time when you are there."

King did not hear it; his ears were turned to Scandinavia where in another sixty days, he would receive the world's greatest humanitarianism award.

Only two other black men had been recipients of the Nobel Peace Prize: Dr. Ralph Bunche in 1950 for arranging the Arab-Israeli peace after the partition of Palestine, and Chief Albert John Luthuli for his unrewarded search for racial peace in South Africa in 1961. Luthuli died in 1967. There had been a question about his even leaving South Africa to accept the prize, but the government relented in the face of an international outcry. After receiving the Nobel Peace Prize, Chief Luthuli returned to the house arrest that had been imposed upon him for his leadership of the African National Congress. He had been confined since 1958 after the "treason trials" that resulted in the Congress' dismemberment.

The Reverend Dr. McCleod Brian had urged King to get in touch with Luthuli as early as October, 1959. Brian told

King that Luthuli's "greatest inspiration" had been King's *Stride Toward Freedom,* smuggled to him by the anti-apartheid Bishop Reeves who later was exiled from South Africa. Luthuli had had to read the book hidden in the cane fields. King then wrote Luthuli, aware his letters would be screened by the officials and was careful, therefore, not to endanger Luthuli. He said in part: "I admire your great witness and your dedication to the cause of freedom and dignity. You've stood amid persecution, abuse and oppression with a dignity and calmness of spirit seldom paralleled in human history."

Now King was flying to stand where Luthuli had stood, and while the United States at that time was not quite like South Africa, many people questioned King's selection for the prize.

The Norwegians and the Swedes, for all their apparent isolation from the mainstream of world events, were nonetheless aware of them. Press reports from Oslo at the time of the Nobel committee's selection mirror a similar ambivalence about King:

Arbeiderbladet, pro labor and government in Norway, said, "A Peace Prize to Martin Luther King will have great effect at an important time for American negroes (*sic*). It will mean a hand proffered to all liberal forces within the American democracy, those now trying to implement the spirit and the idea behind the new civil rights bill (of 1964). The award will also be of importance in the struggle for liberty of colored peoples in other parts of the world."

Aftonposten, conservative and the largest daily said: "If Dr. King fully deserves his award, it is however not so certain that the Nobel Committee does. Its task is to administer a *peace prize,* which is not the same as an award for the advancement of racial rights. . . . It can reasonably be asked what Luthuli has contributed to the work for peace between *nations,* though his work for his own people can only command respect. The parallel between Luthuli and King is striking. . . ."

The left-leaning liberal paper, *Dagbladet,* saw it this way:

"We must be brought to realize that it would mean a real and serious threat to peace—mine, yours and the world's—if the race conflict should really explode into violence. That goes for South Africa and for the U.S. and other countries. . . ."

Heading for his rendezvous with international destiny, or so it was thought, King set out with a party of twenty-six people which included his parents, brother Reverend A. D. King, and sister, secretaries and his strong right arm, Ralph David Abernathy. The party stopped in London where King delivered a sermon in St. Paul's Cathedral. Under the deep nave, surrounded by statues of saints and the heavy neo-Roman architecture, he announced that he would donate the entire sum of the $54,000 Nobel Prize money to civil rights causes, and to a fund to further studies in nonviolence. Then the group of black Americans was on the way to Oslo.

Dark Scandinavian winter clouds dripped rain, but several hundred people waited for the plane which was being delayed because of the weather. They held a sign that read: DR. MARTIN LUTHER KING, JR., BAPTIST YOUNG PEOPLE WELCOME YOU. The reception accorded King was equal to Luthuli's and Dr. Albert Schweitzer's but noisier.

On the eighth of December, *Dagbladet* editorialized as follows:

"We all have reason to be grateful for people of King's type . . . He represents that struggle that can be fought in ways leading to lasting reconciliation, with bridges built and roads to wider fellowship. The Nobelwinner this year is not merely a leader within his own country, but also a symbol of the liberation movement involving hundreds of millions of people . . . If such a man is scorned and *pursued* [italics added] by the FBI chief, the natural question is whether the latter is not ready to be replaced, whereas King's position is in no way weakened."

Unrecorded during King's triumphal tour was the fact that Swedish gypsies led by Katerina Taikom were trying to reach him to convey to him their own desperate and second-class position in Swedish society. They were unsuccessful.

On December 10, dapper in striped pants and cutaway coat, King delivered the address all Nobel winners must give. Behind him sat the orchestra. In the two front seats placed in the center of the aisle were King Olaf V and Crown Prince Harald of Norway. The ceremony was held in Festival Hall of the University of Oslo.

In its spirit King's speech echoed that of another Southern American, who'd won the Nobel Prize for Literature, William Faulkner. Faulkner had said, "I decline to accept the end of man."

King reiterated, "I refuse to accept the idea that man is mere flotsam and jetsam in the river of life . . . I refuse to accept the cynical notion that nation after nation must spiral down a militaristic stairway into the hell of thermonuclear destruction. . . ."

And then: "I have the audacity to believe that peoples everywhere can have three meals a day for their bodies, education and culture for their minds, and dignity for their spirits. I believe that what self-centered men have torn down, other-centered men can build up . . . I still believe that we shall overcome."

Eight

SHORTLY after Kennedy had been murdered in Dallas, Malcolm X made his statement about the "chickens coming home to roost"—or, in other words, that a man gets what he deserves. Elijah Muhammad suspended him and banned him from further public appearances. Up until that time white Americans, through the white communications media, had been lead to believe that the nation's restless blacks had a choice between Malcolm and King. King had, in fact, often observed that he and SCLC were the alternatives to Malcolm and the Black Muslims.

As far as American blacks were concerned, there were no choices to be made; both men were valuable and had their place in the scheme of black things. American whites, on the other hand, to their damnation, rejected both Malcolm and King, seeing little difference between them.

Elijah Muhammad found himself in the strange position of being praised, although faintly and in secret, by whites for his suspension of Malcolm (they had misunderstood the reasons for it in any case). Malcolm, finally severing ties with the Muslims, established his own organization in Harlem. In the conversation I had with him in Lagos in early 1964, it was apparent that the distance that seemed to have existed between himself and King was small indeed, although he never gave up the idea of self-defense for blacks. Malcolm was even willing to sing "We Shall Overcome," just so long as all who were singing had .45's firmly in hand.

Chester Himes, in Spain in 1969, who also knew Malcolm slightly, gave me his view of why Malcolm was dangerous—as dangerous as King—to the American scene:

". . . As long as the white press and the white community keep throwing it out that the black man hates white people, he's safe. It doesn't do a damn thing to him; he can walk around wherever he wishes. Look at Le Roi Jones who stands up there and tells those white people whatever he wants to tell them. Stokely Carmichael, Rap Brown, anybody, they're safe. . . .

"Malcolm X had developed a philosophy in which he included all the peoples of the world, and people were listening to him. And then he became dangerous. Now, as long as he was staying in America and just hating the white man, he wasn't dangerous. But when he involved others, they figured that if he kept on . . . bring in the masses of other people, masses of whites, masses of North Africans, masses of yellow people, all that would make him dangerous. . . ."

It will not go unobserved that both Malcolm and King died as they attempted to mount programs involving not only blacks, but the oppressed of every race and kind.

While Malcolm X was getting his Organization for Afro-American Unity off the ground in New York, in 1964 Martin King turned again to Alabama. Over the years SCLC had been nibbling at it here and there, but George Wallace and the stomp-down crackers had proved to be a formidable obstacle.

Selma, 1965, was to have been the breakthrough. Again there had been a vanguard at work, SNCC, but it had been hindered by Sheriff Jim Clark and by the decisions against it rendered by the prosegregationist state courts. The voter registration drives had been repeatedly blunted, but forces were gathering.

February. School children by the hundreds of thousands looked eagerly forward to the birthdays of Abraham Lincoln and George Washington. The first tentative assaults on Selma began and King, together with Abernathy, went to jail for leading a march of a few whites and over 200 blacks to the courthouse. While they were in jail, SNCC invited Malcolm X to speak before the demonstrators, which he did, leaving town before King and Abernathy were released. Death began stalking the Alabama Black Belt on the nineteenth of February, claiming the life of Jimmie Lee Jackson, who died of a beating he received 20 miles outside Selma. Then death, with overtones of the American eagle at full swoop, went north, and in the Audubon Ballroom in Harlem on February 21, Malcolm X was gunned down. At once his death was attributed to a Black Muslim vendetta, supposedly because they had made so many reported threats on his life. Malcolm himself had seemed to regard at least some of the threats as Muslim-originated.

Near the end of the Civil War Selma had been the target of a raid out of Georgia, and an engagement. Like veterans who've never seen combat, the legends of Selma radically overstate the city's involvement in the war between the states. Perhaps it was so rabidly a cracker stronghold because it had not been wiped off the face of the earth by Union troops.

We have all been taught from childhood that the right to vote is priceless; we withhold that right from ex-convicts, from aliens who have not gone through the naturalization process, and to a large extent from black people living in the South. During Reconstruction when these people, largely ex-slaves, did possess the vote, black political representatives were in both the state and national law-making bodies. Then the vote was withheld so that black people would be politically powerless. In a nation where politics has become the hub of every other American institution, withholding of the ballot effectively excluded them from America in all but their presence at the bottom of the social scale—which was precisely where they had been before 1863.

Voter registration drives in the South had not been altogether successful. White Southerners knew that they could desegregate public transportation systems if they were forced

to, without giving up control of the ballot box. The vote was something else. This, the ballot, if not the mainspring of democracy, was the mainspring of power. This was perhaps the most tangible of the goals to be gained—and the most dangerous.

On March 1, 1965, King led a march through five Alabama Black Belt counties, including Lowndes County where SNCC had formed the Lowndes County Freedom Party, otherwise known as the Black Panther Party (a Negro combat unit in World War I in France had carried that name). Whites gathering behind George Wallace had taken as their symbol the fighting white cock; SNCC responded with the black panther. Stokely Carmichael would rise from the training ground of the rich black fields of Lowndes to become head of SNCC.

Four days after the march, King was in Washington, head-to-head with Lyndon Johnson, pressing for speed in voting rights legislation and in providing for federal registrars to replace the local ones. For a century local registrars in the South had effectively blocked the efforts of blacks to register by confronting them with confusing, unfair questions that, had they been asked them, would have quickly disqualified them from voting, too. SNCC, for a year and a half, had been running headlong into this blockade. Black college professors as well as field hands had been mowed down by registrars who were often just barely literate themselves.

There was a confrontation coming; press people were flying into Alabama from all over the world; supporters of King and his demonstrators were flocking South, too. In Selma, an internal face-off was taking place between Wilson Baker, chief of police, and Sheriff Jim Clark, of Birmingham. Backing up Clark's tough, no-march policy was Colonel Al Lingo of the Alabama Highway Patrol, who had also been at Birmingham. Chief Baker had been handling the SNCC protests with moderation, compared to what black demonstrators were used to at the hands of other law enforcement officials.

Behind the scenes U.S. Attorney General Nicholas Katzenbach and former Florida governor, LeRoy Collins, now head of the federal Community Relations Service, were in contact with King and the White House. The stage seemed to be set, and King announced a march from Selma to the state capitol in Montgomery for Sunday, March 7. Governor Wallace promptly banned the planned march—a ban which was properly ignored since it was another of those "unjust laws" with which black people (and some white people know of them, too) are familiar.

Of laws like this, Alexis de Tocqueville in *Democracy in America* says in the chapter headed "The Tyranny of the Majority": "When I refuse to obey an unjust law, I do not contest the right of the majority to command, but I simply appeal from the sovereignty of the people to the sovereignty of mankind."

Which King was doing.

But not in Selma—instead from his home in Atlanta, where, Miller says, he could "devote his efforts to lining up national support." The Reverend Hosea Williams had been left in charge; Abernathy was with King.

Sunday afternoon in Selma—usually a time for resting after the dinner that follows morning church—was different on March 7. More than 500 marchers led by Hosea Williams, John Lewis, and James Forman, headed for Highway 80, many with packs on their backs and heavy walking shoes on their feet. They wound watchfully past state troopers and a sheriff's posse—those traditional American vigilantes, hustled up by Sheriff Clark. Walking quietly and uneasily, they crossed Edmund Pettus Bridge. On the other side more state troopers, sheriff's deputies, and cracker vigilantes waited. The newsmen were moving among the crowd, and the television cameras were grinding.

A brief exchange of words took place between Hosea Williams and Major John Cloud who gave the marchers two minutes to turn around. There is a question as to whether the two minutes were up when Cloud ordered his troopers forward. But the troopers charged, looking for all the world like a film clip out of World War I in their tin hats—except that the people in front of them were Americans. The troopers on foot, canisters of tear gas hooked onto their belts, their gas masks in place, moved forward with their clubs ready. John Lewis went down; a woman was spewed out of the melee of charging horsemen, and the rout was on.

The rebel yell—that shriek beginning with an almost closed glottis and then rolling murderously from the front of the mouth—echoed again and again above the sound of galloping horses, bursts of tear gas, shouting demonstrators, who were being driven, beaten, and stomped toward the George Washington Carver housing project. Negroes lived in the project, a fact not lost on the crackers, and they proceeded to tear gas the occupants. Chief Baker, who'd had a running jurisdictional dispute with Sheriff Clark and Al Lingo, now took over the maintenance of law and order, but the number of injured among the blacks and whites was close to seventy.

In Atlanta King issued a call for religious leaders the nation over to join in another march from Selma to Montgomery in support of voting rights. Within hours, some clergymen and laymen were arriving in Selma. One of them, the Reverend James Reeb, a white from Boston, was attacked by four crackers and died two days later. The first to die had been Jimmie Jackson; now Reeb.

King and Abernathy rushed to Selma, to conduct services for Reeb. After listening to President Johnson speak the passwords "We shall overcome" (thus Johnson stole King's thunder even more deftly than Kennedy had—this time over national television), they went on to Montgomery to firm up the portrait of movement unity, which was becoming unstuck again. That taken care of, at least publicly, King resumed his demanding schedule of speaking in different parts of the country, and flying back to Selma periodically to keep the campaign there intact.

Splinter demonstrations erupted during the following weeks,

and finally, on another Sunday, March 21, all differences were ironed out between the state and federal courts, between Wallace and Johnson, between King and SNCC. More than 10,000 people took part in the march from Selma to Montgomery, and another 25,000 met them in the capital. The march route was protected by troops—once again. Political, labor, and religious leaders marched in the front ranks, and at Montgomery there was a rally in front of the Dexter Avenue Baptist Church, where King had begun his march across the world headlines. That George Wallace was not in his office to receive the leadership delegation when the first contingents arrived surprised no one.

But the crackers had not given up just because a bunch of "niggers" and "nigger-lovers" had managed to get their march. That evening the mother of five children, Mrs. Viola Liuzzo, was shot to death in her car while ferrying riders back to Selma. As in the case of Reeb's death, the murderer and his accomplices were quickly apprehended. (But no Southerner fears the punishment a Southern court will mete out—if his victim is black or a white Negro-sympathizer.) Three murders, close to 4,000 arrests, interminable court arguments—and only about 50 black people had been added to the voting lists.

But there *was* a Voting Rights Act; it would go into effect later in the year. It was another of those plugs for Constitutional loopholes that would not have been necessary had the Constitution been strictly, speedily, and heartily enforced. But even this plug had a loophole in it; it was to remain in force for five years. It was, therefore, a *temporary* right, surrendered only because power had been demanded to give it up, to paraphrase the words of Frederick Douglass. The act would have to come up for renewal by Congress in 1970—and all United States Congresses have been dominated by Southerners, if not in actual number then in committee and influence power.

The Voting Rights Act was applicable in any county or state in which less than 50 percent of the voting-age population was registered or had voted in the 1964 national election. Literacy tests were done away with, and the U.S. Attorney General was empowered to appoint federal registrars to enforce the provisions of the law. Since the act's passage, four-fifths of the qualifying Southern blacks have registered to vote for the first time: 800,000 souls. And over 50 percent of the eligible Negro population has voted, bringing about significant changes in state legislatures, county, and city offices.

One thinks back to the pre-Reconstruction period when there was black representation from the bottom of the political ladder to the top—and one also thinks of the maneuvers of the Nixon Administration in mid-1969 to curtail these rights gained after such great human expense at Selma in 1965.

Again to refer back to de Tocqueville (and I shouldn't, because he is another of the many historians who viewed America as white and who dealt with the question of slavery,* which has since come to plague the nation as nothing more than an aside), he also believed that the great revolutions "which have changed the aspect of nations" and which were "made to consolidate or to destroy social inequality," were past, because democracies tend to pander to all, satisfying all. But there were 4,000,000 slaves in the nation, and their descendants remain, on the whole, unsatisfied and extremely desirous of their rights as citizens. They wish other Americans to feel as intensely about their rights as they do. De Tocqueville may even have supplied the reason why the majority of whites don't:

"The attachment which men feel to a right and the respect which they display for it, is generally proportioned to its importance, or to the length of time during which they have enjoyed it. The rights of private persons amongst democratic nations are commonly of small importance, or recent growth,

* Although he was in America at the time, and most of the nation sooner or later got word of the Nat Turner Rebellion, for him there was nothing to perceive in or about it.

and extremely precarious; the consequence is, that they are often sacrificed without regret, and almost always violated without remorse. . . . Men become less attached to private rights just when it is most necessary to retain and defend what little remains of them."

On the whole, then, if one is—in 1970—to consider the movement and its aspirations, the gains of Selma might be said to have been minute.

Nine

VOTING rights may have just come too late.
The often slow and tedious move-by-move campaigns of King and SCLC were consuming too much time, and millions of blacks were switching their allegiance to the younger, more realistic leaders who were springing up in every city. It is a cliché, but also axiomatic, that justice delayed is justice solidly denied—and Martin King was not getting enough justice quickly enough for a lot of black people.

Not that he didn't work at it. Each display of "creative tension," in the cities where the national spotlight had been focused because of King, brought him, when the campaigns were over, more invitations to speak before groups all over the nation. He toured Roxbury and spoke to the Massachusetts Legislature in Boston; he was awarded the American Liberties Medal of the American Jewish Committe; he was guest of honor at the commencement exercises at Oberlin College; he spoke to the powerful New York City Central Labor Council, the group that very nearly breaks or makes any mayoralty candidate; he addressed the New York Bar Association and attended—as a noncelebrity—the Congress of the Baptist World Alliance, and his old nemesis, Dr. Joseph Harrison Jackson, was also there.

Tentatively, King flexed his might in the city of the big shoulders, Chicago, on behalf of integrated schooling, better education for black children, and the ouster of school superintendent Benjamin Willis. For nearly two years Willis had been on the hot seat, the target of black parents who saw him as the key stumbling block to decent education for their children. Before King agreed to lend some brief assistance to the school campaign, there had been, if not apathy, fragmented demonstrations and disunity. Quickly he mounted the podiums of Chicago and nearby suburbs and led a march of upward of 20,000 people. When King left Chicago, fragmentation and disunity returned.

Early in August he was back in Washington for the signing of yet another bill he'd been instrumental in getting passed— the 1965 Voting Rights Act. Then he was off to Puerto Rico. Just at the moment when he needed a well deserved rest, the United States was entering upon a new era.

Los Angeles. How does one really describe Nut City? To begin, it was the Chicago of the post-World War II period. Negroes in the South no longer saw the Illinois Central as their sole escape route; increasingly they boarded the westbound trains, too. Many of their relatives had worked in war-related industries, particularly in northern California; perhaps the southern part of the state would open up soon. The key base in the south was Los Angeles.

Others had preceded the blacks: the Okies in the thirties who fled the stifling dust bowls only to be hounded by "native Angeleno" vigilante groups. And the Angelenos weren't alone in their intolerance. Crackers from the South by the hundreds of thousands carried their virulent bigotry over the Rockies to allow it to germinate with the native strain. Californians have an ugly and long-standing history of prejudice in dealing with Mexican-Americans and Asian-Americans; did black people believe they would be treated better?

I have relatives living in Los Angeles, and I lived there for a year myself and had been, as I've said elsewhere, "unemployed for an astronomical number of days." We had lived in the section called Watts.

It so happened that I was in Los Angeles visiting relatives

for the first time in two years, only days before the Watts rebellions broke out. The Black Muslims had been proselytizing with enough success to bring the Los Angeles Police Department to at least one highly publicized, one-sided shoot-out, and a Muslim had been killed. There was a new atmosphere in the black bars and restaurants, a kind of waiting, a kind of had-it-up-to-here attitude. Two things happened to members of my family that highlighted the posture of both black and white communities.

My stepfather was returning from a ball game and, with his visiting brother, stopped in a bar on Imperial Highway. They were served, but as soon as they'd finished, the bartender broke their glasses in that melodramatic, bigoted manner. Several Japanese-Americans who were seated in the place immediately got up and left. My stepfather and his brother left, too. Two days later while my mother and stepfather were watching me on television, two detectives came to their house, were admitted, and promptly began a search; they had no search warrant and my stepfather ordered them out. They promised to come back with one, but never did. He didn't know what they were looking for, and they didn't tell him.

My experiences and my family's experiences plus those of thousands of blacks added up to Watts in August, 1965.

King and Bayard Rustin rushed to Los Angeles—and found themselves catapulted from the fairly orderly world of non-violent protest into the maelstrom of the long-delayed but inevitable violent confrontation of angry and near powerless blacks with frightened but powerful whites, represented in the main by the police department. Also on hand was Dick Gregory, the one star, I am convinced, who *always* puts his money where his mouth is when it comes to black people and their needs.

King had no base in Los Angeles, so his efforts were confined to a walking tour of Watts, an attempt to "reason" with the inhabitants, and an exchange of words with Governor Edmund Brown.

On August 20, while Watts was still in flames, and police bullets were taking their deadly toll, President Johnson publicly compared the rebels of that ghetto to the Ku Klux Klan. It seems he thought the passage of the Voting Rights Act of 1965—signed with great flourish and publicity only two weeks before—was the tranquilizer for all black people for all time. That it did not tranquilize Watts where black people *had* the vote, and often little else, angered him; Santa Claus' gift didn't fit the sock.

If Watts angered Johnson, it puzzled King. He had had to ask Louis Lomax, who lived in Los Angeles at the time, what caused the explosion. Watts should have been considered a prelude to what would happen during his Chicago campaign a year later, in the summer of 1966. There was a vast difference between the mechanics of race and politics in the South and North, a difference King seems to have ignored. Generally, though, black people in both regions agreed on a most important consideration—freedom.

A few years ago, Earl Burrus Dickerson, president of the Supreme Life Insurance Company of America of Chicago, which is black-owned and services mainly black clients, said to me: "There's no power on earth that can keep the Negro from full citizenship in this country; he'll either get it or there will be a holocaust."

Dickerson, a resident of Chicago from his boyhood, and a holder of numerous prestigious positions within the establishment as well as in the black community, was seventy-five when he made that statement; seventy-five and considered to be one of the few black millionaires.

The Southern Christian Leadership Council in cooperation with the Chicago-based Coordinating Council of Community Organizations set up operations for the Windy City. CCCO's function had been to make the people who lived in slum neighborhoods aware of their plight. Once aware, the theory went, they could then begin to act. By and large, however, these areas in Chicago were heavily populated with Negroes not too many years out of the South, and "swinging" Chicago tended to anesthetize their awareness of their situation. The differences between King's campaigns in the urban North and the urban South, therefore, can't be underlined often enough.

In the South, for all its hereditary weaknesses, the church remained a rallying point for blacks about to mount their demonstrations. In the North (east *and* west) that strength was diminished because the churches were not cultural as well as religious centers; there were many other competing forces, preoccupations and entertainments that drew the people away from full-time involvement with the church.

In the South, black people were systematically excluded from any participation in the political system, which inevitably meant economic power. Some blacks, like the insurance moguls, did achieve economic independence by serving the black community. The North was different. In Chicago, black people to an extent deemed safe and sufficient by white politicians, were a part of the political system. Congressman William Dawson, for example, is believed to possess considerable power in the black neighborhoods of Chicago, even though he is often accused of either misusing it or not using it at all; most of all he is charged with being a tool of the Daley machine.

Generally, the Chicago press had reservations about the SCLC campaign; the goings-on in the South were all right, but what, after all, did King hope to achieve in a city where, as Lionel Lokos says in *House Divided* (Arlington House, 1968), there was not "a single segregation law on its books." Of the black press, the Chicago *Defender,* once the most important newspaper black people could lay hands on across the nation, had pulled in its horns and was now local in character but still considered to be militant.

The largest and most influential black press publications are issued by the Johnson Publishing Company; *Ebony* and *Jet* are the major magazines, but in recent years *Negro Digest* has become the guidepost of militant intellectuals. Its circulation, however, is much smaller than *Ebony* and *Jet*. Very little was mentioned of King's campaign in either of these two magazines. Lerone Bennett, Jr., a senior editor and historian-author, in his book on King, *What Manner of Man*, has but one note on Chicago in the index and that refers to the Chicago *Sun-Times*. Yet his book was published by Johnson. The memorial story in *Ebony* by Phyl Garland, that appeared after King's murder, refers to the Chicago campaign only in the caption of a single photo. The *Jet* memorial issue of April 18, 1968, makes two references to King in Chicago. (The *Ebony* Picture Biography of King, on the other hand, includes a number of photos of King taken there.)

No sooner had it been announced that King was coming to Chicago to stump for open housing than the television people got busy, rounded up some black ministers, who appeared to be jacklegs, and recorded their opposition to the campaign.

Chicago was also the home base of Dr. Joseph Harrison Jackson, King's long-time critic and a man who had great praise for the American system, a man who believed that it was possible that the civil rights movement was of interest to people *outside* the United States. ("I believe the Negro has been used by persons with interests contrary to the best interests of the United States," he said in *Human Events* in October, 1966.)

Negro clergymen were not the only clerics who opposed King; Catholic monsignors would bless the medals of white toughs out to stone King as he passed through their neighborhoods. In 1969, John Cardinal Cody, archbishop of Chicago, would be described by one of his black priests as "unconsciously racist." Then there were the politicians, particularly the hundreds of local officials who tend to regard Mayor Richard Daley as the bossman.

Most of all King was going into a Chicago where the hopes and aspirations of the black people at that time were radically splintered. In a decade the population had boomed, from just over half a million to beyond a million. The traditional southside ghetto, semighetto and nonghetto, could no longer contain the black influx, and so it veered to the west, into buildings and areas already in the last stages of decay. Yet hope was still in the air; for black people in America hope has been the bone always held in front of the dog, who even as he pursues it finds that he cannot reach it—the distance is forever fixed. Still who knows, the string might snap, the bone might slip from its noose. But in Chicago hope was running out— slowly, but going nonetheless.

Martin King was a part-time Chicagoan. The Chicago campaign was handled on a day-to-day basis by James Bevel, Andy Young, Jesse Jackson, and Hosea Williams. (Wyatt Tee Walker had left SCLC, but would remain close to it.) While in Chicago, King actually lived in a slum tenement to order to draw even closer attention to the work of the Union to End Slums. (But the apartment had been painted and refurbished for him by UES people.) Several times during the campaign, which had got off the ground in January, he left Chicago, first for Europe, then for SCLC's convention, held that year in Miami, and for New York, Alabama, Washington, and Hollywood to raise funds, to receive awards, and to make known what was going on in Chicago. All efforts there were going to climax in a massive End Slums Rally and Freedom Festival on July 10.

Some 1,500 miles to the south, another black Southerner was preparing to embark on a lonely pilgrimage; he would have no entourage and no headlines. His journey and what would happen on it would bring him to a meeting with Martin King. The pilgrim's name was James Meredith.

While Meredith was preparing to walk the Southern highways and Martin King was readying the climax of the Chicago campaign, my wife Lori and I were in Europe. We had spent six months in Spain where I was working on a novel, and our plan was to spend another six months in Amsterdam where the book was partially set. We left Spain at the end of May and drove to Florence to visit friends. After a few days we headed for Amsterdam, arriving there Monday, June 7. The following day, while we were dining with friends, we learned that Meredith had been shot while walking through his home state, Mississippi. We did not know then if he was dead or alive. I was plagued by a sense of dread.

I had met Meredith, as I had met Malcolm X, in Nigeria. In fact, I was in Nigeria a second time when word came that Malcolm had been murdered. Now, I thought, Meredith. He had appeared on a television show with me in Nigeria, and later visited me in Lagos (he was based in Ibadan). Still later he was my houseguest when I was living in the Chelsea section of Manhattan. James Meredith is a "spooky" man. His vision is set on horizons invisible to most of us. He asks advice only so he can reject it. Meredith and I had corresponded while Lori and I were back in Spain. He'd said nothing about his march.

The next day we learned that Meredith had not been killed, and a new set of feelings rushed in. His book, *Three Years in Mississippi* (Indiana University Press, 1966), had not been well received. He had complained to me about the lack of publicity. I felt that his lonely pilgrimage was to garner publicity for himself and his book.

For all that, I was deeply shocked by the report of the shooting. There are very few of us who do not feel that what happened at the University of Mississippi in the summer of 1962 helped to make Meredith the man he is today. His experience there is an accelerated version of what happens to every black person in the United States, sometimes subtly, often in slow motion. And there are few of us who would have braved what Meredith braved, just for an education in the state in which his family had lived for some seven generations.

Meredith's shooting sent shock waves through the nation. The leaders of SCLC, CORE, SNCC, NAACP, the National

Urban League, burned up the telephone wires talking to one another. Could they now ignore what Meredith had been trying to do—prove that a black man could walk the highways in safety? Was this not an opportune time to try to forge an appearance of unity again?

As Meredith lay in the hospital, the movement organizations became convinced that the Meredith march had to be continued, and it was, from the point near Hernando, Mississippi, where Meredith—turning toward the concealed voice calling his name, only to receive shotgun pellets in the head— had gone down.

We talked about that march and Martin King, James Meredith and I, early in 1969. We sat in a small room that served him as an office. He owned the building where we talked, and as a preface to our conversation about King, he told me that he would probably be cited as a slumlord because he was having trouble with his white tenants.

He had grown heavier since I last saw him, and his speech, always deliberate, was even more slow to come. When had he first met King? Nine students from Tougaloo had sat-in at a white library. The sit-in had gained support from other students, and King had come to Jackson, Mississippi, to lend his prestige to their efforts. "That was before he was well known, 1960 or 1961." That seemed strange, because King was extremely well known at that time. "So I heard about him coming," Meredith continued, "and I drove out to the airport to meet him. No one else had gone to meet him. He wasn't very happy standing out there at the airport all alone."

We moved to the march. Movement leaders came to visit Meredith in the hospital. "They all came, and really, didn't any of them have any choice. A new direction of the whole movement moved from there. The march started after I was shot and because I was shot. I was the symbol of the thing."

Somewhat bitterly Meredith recalled: "Everybody knew I was going on the walk before I went. Not only did no one go, nobody even mentioned it. Then Stokely Carmichael's stature increased as a result of the march, also McKissick's, but Carmichael's mostly. But I was the central figure in the whole thing. I couldn't call the shots, but nobody could do anything opposite the shots I called."

I didn't question the contradiction. An interview with Meredith (this was my second) is a taxing situation, and the interviewer, once he has begun, wishes he hadn't. But many of Meredith's observations were worth waiting for. For example, he was surprised at the "lack of control and discipline even among his [King's] own people" on the march.

Meredith asked him if it had always been that way, and King answered that the discipline was better then than it usually was. "That explains why things are in such a lull now," Meredith said to me. "I believe in one general."

To support Meredith, time and time again King was charged with being a poor organizer, a man who couldn't keep order among his aides in SCLC. Meredith with his long years in the Air Force recognized this flaw at once.

It was on the Meredith march that the slogan, black power, was said to have been born. According to King in *Where Do We Go From Here* (Harper & Row, 1967) Stokely Carmichael, credited with originating the phrase said, "Martin, I deliberately decided to raise this issue on the march in order to give it a national forum and force you to take a stand for black power."

King laughed. "I have been used before," he said. "One more time won't hurt."

Like many others, King first feared the phrase; his fear had an altogether different base, however. He did not want to alienate white support, and the words were a challenge to be hurled into the faces of whites—who at this point were not entirely welcome in SNCC anyway. Carmichael was representative of many of the young black leaders. He had been in his teens when the Supreme Court decision was handed down in 1954. James Baldwin writes: "Did they really suppose that fifteen-year-old black boys remain fifteen forever?" Carmichael, like others his age, had been attracted to the movement by the initial work of King and SCLC. The very name of the organization he headed is proof that once, *once* the members of the Student Nonviolent Coordinating Committee believed in the efficacy of peaceful protest. They had, however, become thoroughly disenchanted with it.

The split between the oldsters in SCLC (also the NAACP and the Urban League—CORE, with Floyd McKissick, sided with SNCC) was now very evident. For the youngsters, nonviolence was out; for the youngsters, white liberalism was only bigotry in slow motion.

Meredith rejoined the march that had had such considerable trouble with the Mississippi crackers. *"My* march," Meredith told me. As with other marches, this one was to end at the state capitol in Jackson, and it did, but 200 feet away from it. The march was over. The state of Mississippi resumed its main business—the oppression of black people. I suppose that when you are the poorest state in the union, you have to do something to feel important.

Martin King flew back to Chicago to lead the 45,000 marchers in the End Slums Rally and Freedom Festival from Soldiers Field to City Hall to present Mayor Richard Daley with proposals dealing with school integration and budgets, improved municipal transportation to provide better service in the black neighborhoods, strict regulation of lending institutions that had unjustifiably refused Negroes mortgage loans, and the construction of low-rent housing units. Having delivered the proposals, King turned his attention to the marches planned to move through white neighborhoods.

On one of those marches King and his demonstrators walked through a mob composed of "ethnics," members of the American Nazi Party, and "komrades" of the local Ku Klux Klan. King was hit with a brick, and the mob, screaming for black blood, almost got it.

The target of that well-aimed brick was also a Nobel Peace

Prize winner. In other nations, with the conspicuous exception of South Africa, this meant something, something having to do with the efforts of all people who are bound together on this earth living in peace. That Martin King won the award augured well for the American possibility of gaining racial peace; that Americans failed to recognize this has damned them to a restless racial future—which they well deserve and, in fact, have long deserved.

Al Capone's town, Cicero, Illinois, was the spot next picked to bring the Chicago officials to an agreement on the points King had submitted on July 10. Black people have had it hard in Cicero, as hard as in any Deep South "stomp-down" cracker town. As in Dearborn, Michigan, north of Detroit, a Negro was far better off not to be found in Cicero after dark unless he had business there, and often even that didn't guarantee his safety.

White people know exactly how vicious other white people can be, and the prospect of a march on Cicero was completely unpalatable. I've always been convinced that the reason for the silence of what used to be called the "moderates" is that they, being white, are more aware of white viciousness than the blacks. It has been amply demonstrated that whites involved in civil rights demonstrations can expect the utmost fury of the mob to be turned upon them as "traitors." Reverend James Reeb, Mrs. Viola Liuzzo, and Goodman and Schwerner are the names that come most quickly to mind as victims of white rage.

Thus ostensibly because of the tension in Cicero, the Chicago Commission on Religion and Race called a conference two days before the march was to take place, and an agreement of sorts was hammered out. Young people involved in the demonstrations declared that King had sold out—a cry he'd heard before after Selma—but he calmly pronounced the agreement as "most significant."

It had been a strange campaign. Archbishop Cody, for example, had gone with King on a march through a white neighborhood. (Later he was called an "unconscious racist" by a black priest.) Mayor Daley on one hand insisted to the press that there was nothing wrong with Chicago, but on the other hand shared the dais with King when the final agreement was reached. Daley also had implied that the police files revealed that some of King's marchers were Communists and that Communist money was helping to finance the demonstrations.

But, for all practical purposes, the Chicago campaign was about over.

In October, 1966, back from Europe only a week, I took off for Chicago to do a piece on black families in the lower, middle, and upper classes. I've known Chicago since I was almost eighteen and have many friends and relatives living there. For the first time in all those years, *people in every class were talking alike;* a welfare mother, a vice-principal, and a millionaire. I think Martin King was responsible for that.

Ten

As 1966 neared its end, Johnson's war in Vietnam shared the headlines with black power. Interpretations of the latter were spurious, designed to sell newspapers and magazines, attract television viewers, and to sever the final, tenuous ties existing between black and white.

In *Where Do We Go From Here,* King set out to define black power, citing first the incongruity of a nonviolent movement at home which is applauded by whites who are conducting a war in Vietnam. He viewed it too as being a call to black people "to amass the political and economic strength to achieve their legitimate goals." Finally he saw it as a "psychological call to manhood."

Now this is what the SNCC kids had meant, even if they hadn't verbalized it for the public. I don't doubt at all that these points and perhaps others *were* elucidated for the press, which chose to ignore them in favor of its own interpretations. Like the kids, King saw the need for the accrual of power to effect change in the ghetto.

Black power cut through all the bullshit. White people knew at once what was meant, for they had utilized white ethnic power from the moment they got off the goddamn boat. Black power was *not* about raping white wives and daughters, it was at the heart of something of *far greater value:* power and the status quo. And the Negroes were talking about *change.* A change in the black condition made mandatory a change in the white condition, for no white man, no matter how far removed he thinks he is from it, has gained what he has, without stepping over the backs, souls, and minds of black people.

Years ago James J. Kilpatrick, the editor of the Richmond, Virginia, *News Leader* and James Baldwin were in a head-to-head debate on television. Kilpatrick began by asking this question: "What have Negroes contributed to Western civilization?"

I jumped up screaming at the set, "Slave labor and cheap labor, Jimmy Blood, man!"

I don't remember Baldwin's answer, probably because it was disappointing. But Kilpatrick, who in November, 1960, was also to debate with King, was assured by Baldwin's answer that black people had not in fact built skyscrapers, produced Van Gogh or Renoir or Gauguin. Neither did the pharoahs build the pyramids. Slavery and the slave trade produced the raw material, easily convertible into currency, that spurred the economic development not only of America but of Mr. Kilpatrick's entire blessed Western civilization.

All of America's fabled institutions, *all* of them, sprang into being or were affected by the presence of black people here; they served as the springboard for unlimited white power, and black power simply meant that white people would not be jumping off *that* springboard anymore.

As Kennedy and Johnson had neatly lifted King's thunder on occasion, King, by defining black power in the realm of semantics most people could have understood had they tried, was letting the air out of the black power bogeyman—or trying to. But, Carmichael, Rap Brown, the press—all seemed bent on leaving the phrase just where it lay on that Mississippi highway.

The presence, the viability of the phrase, however, was all that mattered; within a year the ghettos would be resounding with the labors—intellectual, spiritual and physical—of a gathered and still gathering black people who, at last, it seemed, had found one another.

There was another sizzling issue. Black people had been led to believe that they were only tangentially involved in the Vietnam War, when, in fact, black soldiers were carrying more than their share of the burden. Like the realtor in Montana, some whites said, "It's about time," but that statement was tantamount to admitting that they knew nothing about the history of the black soldier in the United States Army.

King had briefly spoken out against the war, narrowing down his remarks to relate to the Negro and what the fighting meant to him. In May, 1966, Dr. Spock and Yale Chaplain William Sloane Coffin offered to a throng of 15,000 a statement by King in opposition to the war, and as the Chicago campaign and the Meredith march progressed during the year, he spoke out even more strongly against our involvement. (". . . the promises of the Great Society have been shot down on the battlefield of Vietnam"). His presence in the White House was no more. Black people wondered why he was "messing around" with Vietnam when things were in such disrepair back home.

My personal view is that King realized that he *was* a Nobel Peace Prize winner and as such had an obligation to all people. He was an American and the Vietnam War would have been nonexistent without Americans. I also feel that Bayard Rustin, who was always behind the scenes during King's trek through history, unknowingly had much to do with King's stand. For a great many years Rustin was director of the War Resisters League, and is now on the board of that organization as well as the director of the A. Philip Randolph Institute in New York. A Quaker, Rustin has said, ". . . the law of violence is such that each side becomes equally vicious. To try to distinguish between which is more vicious is to fail to recognize the logic of war. It is war that is evil, not the Viet Cong, not the United States."

Besides Rustin, there was a growing awareness among those close to King that the Vietnam War went hand in hand—had to go hand in hand—with his nonviolent philosophy. Diane

Nash Bevel, the wife of the Reverend James Bevel, went to North Vietnam in December. Bevel had become one of King's chief aides. Like many others, Mrs. Bevel had been drawn to King's activities through the sit-ins, and was a leader of them while a student at Fisk University in Nashville.

While the American press was belaboring the "new brotherhood" blacks and whites appeared to have found in Vietnam, the other side of the coin only showed more racism exercised by white soldiers even on the battlefield. The European press revealed this from time to time, and occasionally members of the American press slipped, briefly alluding to shoot-outs between black and white soldiers, then blacking out the details. King's decision to involve himself deeply in the war was undoubtedly founded in part on some of these reports which could not be substantiated, mostly because the press here refused to do so. (It would take until late 1968 and early 1969 for Americans at home to realize that white soldiers had transferred their attitudes from these shores to Vietnam's. Race rebellions would take place in "The Nam.")

Martin King had agreed to serve as a cochairman of Clergy and Laymen Concerned About Vietnam. And there were contradictions aplenty for him to tackle in this arena. The "cruel irony" of the war, as King saw it, was that it took "the black young men who had been crippled by our society and [sent] then 8,000 miles away to guarantee liberties in Southeast Asia which they had not found in Southwest Georgia and East Harlem." King would speak these words in what may have been his greatest speech, April 4, 1967, at Riverside Church, New York City.

But, earlier, in January, it was apparent that King had lost favor not only in the press, but among the public; he no longer numbered among the Gallup Poll's first ten most admired persons.

It is often true that sometimes the best in a man can come out with a dip in his fortunes, and King's had dipped. As they did, however, his view seemed to expand. From love between black and white he went to love between nations; from racism at home, he now seemed to see it washing the world's shores. Although black people were initially cool to the Vietnam situation, they heated up very quickly when the ratio of black soldiers killed to white soldiers killed was played in the press ("military brotherhood" again), and began to listen to King.

It has been my experience that the closer a black man comes to the truth of America in his writing and speaking, the more quickly, the more positively does the nation's press close the doors against him. King's *Time To Break Silence* speech at Riverside Church revealed a man in the process of breaking his own shackles. The speech was replete with the details of American involvement in Southeast Asia; it was a speech that, perhaps for the first time, gave us an American Nobel Prize winner in the role of international peacemaker. That talk had followed by only ten days another Vietnam speech in Chicago. King was building up steam.

On West Fortieth Street in Manhattan, however, the NAACP headquarters, Roy Wilkins and other members of the board, were trying to limit King's role in American life to that of a civil rights leader. Ralph Bunche, who had walked in the front rank with King on the Selma march, along with several other prominent Americans, also felt that King had overstepped his domain.

Even as blacks and whites were stomping King, however, other whites saw him as a Presidential candidate for 1968; Lyndon Johnson had bowed out on Sunday, March 31, utilizing prime time on television, giving Robert Kennedy a lift in his efforts to gain the nomination, and by announcing so late, giving Hubert Humphrey a handicap he was never to overcome. Throughout the nation there was a weariness with the Democrats; only McCarthy seemed to be capable of picking up points, but those who worked with him said he was lazy and relied too much on intellectuals who were political ama-

teurs rather than on the pros like Davey Garth, Tom Morgan,*
and Tom Finney.

So there was a faint, indeed purely wishful hope that with
everything a mess, who knew but that King might sneak
through? But King firmly turned down the overtures.

April 15, 1967. Saturday. We were hosts to friends from
Boston who'd come to town to take part in the march planned
by the Spring Mobilization Committee. Dr. Benjamin Spock
and the Reverend Dr. Martin Luther King, Jr., were to be
the march leaders, together with other religious and civil
rights leaders.

As I am opposed to war and wars, I marched along with my
wife who has similar views. Our friends from Boston had left
to walk with other Beantowners, and my wife and I were
joined by Mrs. Diane Groman, a friend. Since I indicated
earlier that I have low enthusiasm for marches, I might say
now that I went because it was in New York, and because I
thought I might be able to get some interesting photographs.

The march started from Central Park; it was gray and
drizzling. On my back I had a knapsack in which there were
sandwiches for the three of us. The knapsack drew the attention of a young black man who fell in beside us as we started
off. We introduced ourselves, and he gave us his name. He
stayed with us throughout the march, and I had no doubts
whatsoever that he was a cop or an agent.

On Fifty-ninth Street, across from the Plaza Hotel, the egg-
throwers were busy, tossing their little bombs over the heads
of the cops into our ranks. At Lexington Avenue and Fifty-
ninth Street, the workmen from Queens and New Jersey (they
all seem to come from places like that) rained epithets—and
a lethal shower of nails—down on the heads of the marchers,
old and young, black and white alike. Along the route, I could
see police on the rooftops. When we got to UN Plaza, I noticed

*Now Mayor John V. Lindsay's press secretary.

that a group of kids were harassing marchers, and I spoke to a cop, saying that the kids were in the process of creating something the cops were there to prevent. This is what the cop told me: "It's a free country. Besides, they're not wearing beards and sandals like some of you people."

When I returned home late in the afternoon, people were still massed in Central Park waiting to begin the march. As at the March on Washington, the number of people involved was substantially diminished by the police. It was said that 125,000 took part in the Spring Mobilization March, a quarter of a million at Washington. The (low) numbers game serves to keep people on the sidelines who would otherwise be tempted to join. The game also serves to give aid and comfort to the enemies of such efforts, just as the oft-quoted figure of 22,000,000 black people gives authorities the notion that such a number can be handled, if need be, with little more than minimum effort. (The fact, however, is that *black* demographers place the black population at more than 30,000,000, thus equal to and perhaps exceeding the population of Spain, for example.) *

It was clear after that day that while King may have lost ground in some quarters, he was still a figure to contend with. Not since the 1963 March on Washington had he been able to pull together such a coalition of black and white, and this one was far and away mostly white. To be sure, the issue of the war was of itself enough to have drawn so many people, but the fact that it drew two people who were primarily concerned with other things—Dr. Spock with medicine and King with civil rights—was indicative of the seriousness of the issue.

Now King was in his last year, and it was a dangerous one, for what King was moving rapidly toward was political integration of black and white—and mostly, as I've said, white— that was designed to bring an end to the war. The Vietnam

* The U.S. Census Bureau has admitted that it has undercounted the black population by "ten per cent."

issue was the catalyst for the formation of a new populist party.

The status quo in this nation is maintained by keeping the poor, poor, and buying off those who would threaten the position of the rich with niches as managers or other jobs that satisfy. It is the rich who subsidize the middle class because they need a buffer between themselves and the 40-odd million American poor. Today's hard-line white talk of law and order, meaning simply the repression of blacks and other political dissenters, is a result of the middle class' chilling perception that they live in a very tenuous position.

But here came Martin King, coalescing the war-weary. What would come next?

Next came Newark and four days of rebellion lasting from July 12 to July 16, and panic hit the meeting house of the managers of the rich, the Congress of the United States (I exclude some Congressmen, of course). It passed an antiriot bill; it laughed down a proposal to rid the nation of rats on the twentieth of July. Three days later, the black people in Detroit, new riot bill and all, laughter at rats and all, got out and did their thing, which also lasted four days. In both riots it was clear that the police were serving as executioners of black people, therefore, King did himself little good when he approved the use of troops in the rebellious areas.

Even as smoke hung over Newark and Detroit, the first Black Power Conference was called; it was almost fitting that it met in the ashes of Newark—almost, because the battle score was 21 black dead to 2 white dead. In Detroit, 10 whites died along with 33 blacks.

After the rebellions followed repressive laws whipped quickly together, then more white force followed by black rebellion—the cycle was in spiral. As white liberals vanished over the horizon, the black middle class returned to the ghetto if not in body, in spirit.

That summer, after Newark and Washington, I was touring the country again as part of a magazine assignment, this time to assess the mood of the black middle class. It had changed dramatically from my tour in 1963; there was a fired up militancy about it. And this, of course, is natural. People in the middle class have had or are having their brush with the white man in areas and in ways the black in the inner city cannot imagine—although it all amounts to the same thing. I wrote about this new militancy, which was not precisely what the magazine had in mind, and so the piece was not accepted. One editor became angry because some of the black people lived in better homes than he did and he consequently could not understand why they were becoming so militant.

But because there was this spiral and because of the growing role of the middle class, King, at the tenth annual conference of SCLC, hoping to avert even worse rebellion in 1968, offered a program of "massive civil disobedience," hoping to channel rage into something useful. He also feared that Congress was turning its back on the Negro; that the temper of the nation was such that the very existence of black people here was in jeopardy.

Out of these considerations at the end of 1967 came the final plan for the Poor People's March (which Bayard Rustin called in his initial memo, Spring Protest).

This was to be a mammoth undertaking, and not only in terms of numbers, for artificial divisions had long been created and nurtured between the poor of different races. Now, King and perhaps the 100 SCLC workers were going to organize a march, a protest of as many of America's poor as they could reach—the poor Mexican-Americans, poor Puerto Rican-Americans, poor black Americans, poor white Americans, and poor red Americans. In only a matter of months, King hoped to tear down the walls between them and the reservations they themselves had about him, the protest itself, and just the irritating, age-old reluctance about being led by a black man.

But if he could pull it off, a grass-roots populist movement seemed possible. The poor of this nation, forever to their detriment, have never been united; when it seemed back in the twenties and thirties that they were going to be, the rich called off their cops, soft-pedaled that old battle cry of *Reds!*, and allowed the trade labor unions to organize. For hard-core populists, that loomed as a mistake, for not all the poor were absorbed into the unions. As for the unions themselves, they very quickly became part of the establishment, and the dream ended as workers, with a chicken in each of their pots—indeed, with power boats and two cars—quickly moved to slam the door to the good life behind them.

Perhaps no alarm would have been raised had not Lyndon Johnson and John Kennedy before him promised programs to the neglected poor in their New Frontier and Great Society. Both programs, of course, failed to deliver as quickly or as much as was necessary. The poor, whatever their color, were frustrated and disgusted; they'd been had, one-two. And they were discovering that it was *their* sons who were going to Vietnam, because they, as poor parents, had no pull—had no funds to send their sons to college, in effect to buy them student deferments.

It may be true that black soldiers reenlist twice as frequently as white soldiers because they find "more democracy in the Army than in civilian life." But a lot of poor, nonblack soldiers also reenlist for the same reason.

The rich were pulling away from the poor faster than ever, with the cost of living rising steadily since the end of World War II—and vast numbers of the poor were existing on modest annual incomes. It is a sad commentary to consider that, with wealth abounding in the land, the relief programs, somewhat improved since the Depression, were being reinstituted in the 1960's. The only time most Americans even heard about the Food Stamp program was when the recipients bellowed that they did not provide enough.

Other people before King had advocated the establishment of a guaranteed annual income—but no one had planned to gather the poor in Washington to demand it.* As the march was being mobilized, the threat posed the unskilled poor by the technological age became increasingly apparent; machines, computers, would replace even more warm bodies in the nation's factories. There were few signs that the government was capable of seeing to it that there was full employment. The young, sick of the farms anyway because the nation was urban-oriented, found a good excuse to leave them when the machines kept coming. Nationwide interstate road building utilized a few select companies. Transportation emphasis shifted from trains to air, eliminating many of the rail crews and bolstering employment for the technically trained. Old white women and young black women took over the department stores; the young white women had moved up in class or were involved in the new technology in one way or another. White nurses in many hospitals virtually vanished, to be replaced by black ones, themselves well on the way to the middle class.

For the poor, the racially oppressed, no shifts were taking place, no movement at all. In fact their very existence was being denied. Robert Kennedy claimed there were 40,000,000 undernourished or malnourished or starving poor (President Nixon was to claim in 1969 that there were only 16,000,000). It was imperative for the poor to catch up, not only for themselves, but for the nation. The Europeans have learned from the old Romans what Americans refuse to learn: "So many slaves, so many foes."

Out of the many discussions about the Poor People's March came a memo from Bayard Rustin dated January 29, 1968; he had been involved in many of the talks. Rustin was fast losing favor with the younger civil rights people. Like King,

---

* In 1932 the "Bonus Army"—20,000 veterans of World War I—descended on Washington in the depths of the Depression to demand the second half of a bonus voted to them by Congress. Most were driven from their quarters in Anacostia Flats by the Army under General Douglas MacArthur and a young Dwight D. Eisenhower.

he had supported Johnson and then Humphrey. In labor circles he was still the top black man in the United States to deal with, and he could throw his weight to any cause he elected with good effect. But he had had, and was still having, trouble with the younger men on King's staff, like Hosea Williams.

Rustin gave me the carbon of his memo to Martin King, and although parts of it have been published before, I think here it should run in its entirety. The memo is geared to Strategy and Tactics.

I. AIMS AND OBJECTIVES

I submit that the aims and objectives should center on economic questions since I believe that the lack of income is the most serious problem for Negroes. The aim should be stated in two ways: (1) those things not necessarily expected to be achieved now, such as guaranteed income for those who cannot work and public works at decent wages with possibility of upgrading for those who can work (emphasis on the passing of the O'Hara bill); (2) for realizing demands around jobs, housing, welfare, and passage of a strong civil rights bill.

A failure to achieve some major victories in the nation's capital at this time will, I believe, increase frustration nationally. Thus, demands should be broad enough to insure some of them being won soon.

II. BASIC APPROACH

Given the mood in Congress, given the increasing backlash across the nation, given the fact that this is an election year, and given the high visibility of a protest movement in the nation's capital, I feel that any effort to disrupt transportation government buildings, etc., can only lead, in this atmosphere, to further backlash and repression.

Such tactics will, I believe, fail to attract persons dedicated to nonviolence, but, on the other hand, attract elements that cannot be controlled and who, on the contrary, will converge on the project with a variety of objectives in mind other than those of civil rights.

Given this position, I would hope that the spring protest will be limited to constitutional, nonviolent protest.

III. THE STATEMENT OF AIMS & OBJECTIVES

I do not believe it is possible to attract sufficient numbers to the nation's capital unless, far in advance, the strategy and tactics have fully been made clear to all concerned. We are not now in the period we were in 1963, at the time of Selma, Birmingham, and the March on Washington, when there was absolute clarity in everyone's mind as to objectives.

Under those circumstances, people were willing to come when they were called because they did have a clear view that public accommodations and voting rights were of utmost importance. The confusion today around economic questions and the splintering in the movement requires, I am convinced, a clear statement as to objectives, strategy and tactics.

If nonviolent protest within the law is to be used exclusively, or if disruption is to be used, most people not only have a moral right but will insist on having clarification of this point before they will come. The alternative to this clarification is to attract the most irresponsible and uncontrollable elements.

IV. STEPS PRIOR TO THE
WASHINGTON DEMONSTRATION

Not only do I feel it is essential that those being called into Washington know precisely what they are being called into, but I believe it is important that those in Government should have a clear picture of aims, strategy and tactics. I would therefore propose the following steps prior to the Washington demonstration:

(1) Since Walter Washington ("Mayor of Washington") is a Negro and has had limited time to bring about a number of the changes he has in mind, I believe it is imperative for you to meet with him and to discuss where there can be cooperation around certain of his objectives.

(2) As in the March on Washington, I believe you and your staff should have a conference on strategy, tactics and aims with the heads of those departments in Government such as HEW,

Department of Labor, etc., to lay before them the demands and to make quite clear to them the nature of the protest.

(3) Again, as in the March on Washington, I believe you should present the entire program to the leaders of Congress. You will recall that a Republican from the Senate and a Democrat from the House invited to the Senate Caucus Room the liberal congressmen, where Mr. Randolph had the opportunity to explain the aims and objectives of the March on Washington some six weeks prior to the March. That meeting had a very creative effect on the situation.

(4) I believe you should address a series of mass meetings across the country outlining clearly your plans, in order to set the tone for the Washington demonstration in advance so that certain elements would have no excuse for converging on Washington without clarity. I sincerely believe that unless this is done many individuals could become severe problems once they are in Washington.

(5) I am convinced that you should spend at least ten days in Washington, D.C. itself, walking the streets, talking with people and clarifying the strategy and tactics.

V. A POSSIBLE FIRST PROJECT

In order to insure a disciplined and massive first project, I would propose that your staff locate across the country five hundred ministers who are prepared to come to Washington for the first project, with each minister responsible to bring with him ten persons that he can control and who, thus, will be responsible to the discipline that SCLC establishes.

I believe that the first concentration should not be upon government agencies but upon Congress itself and that the slogans and approach should be directed to the failure of Congress to be sensitive to, and to meet the needs. I say this since no city in the country, including Washington, D.C. has the funds, without Congressional assistance, to deal with the problems of housing, education and jobs.

VI. CONCLUSION ON OVER-ALL STRATEGY

There is in my mind a very real question as to whether SCLC can maintain a control and discipline over the April Demonstration even if the methods used are limited to constitutional and nonviolent tactics.

SCLC essentially lost control over the Mississippi march when splintering and confusion was quite simple as compared to the current mood.

I, therefore, feel that the statement attributed to you that in event of violence on the part of your participants you would call off the demonstration is exceedingly a wise decision.

Rustin's assessment of the situation turned out to be tragically true, and this, of course, following his resignation from the PPM when his fears were becoming apparent, further alienated him from the young SCLC aides. Rustin would later become involved in the New York City teacher's strike in the spring of 1968, on the issue of "due process" for the teachers when, in reality, the strike was one more racial issue centering on black community control. This last, plus statements suspiciously reminiscent of the "law and order" programs to combat campus demonstrations, made many Rustin fans wonder if, finally, the events of the day had overtaken him and passed him by.

Eleven

THE early immigrants to America, the adventurers, explorers, indentured servants, charter-holders, and crooks, liked things ancient. They named their slaves Cato and Pompey and Caesar (which they usually spelled Seasor) and Ulysses; they named their cities Utica, Ithaca, and Memphis.

Memphis was a stop on the way out of the South, a blessed relief after being in a city like, for example, Jackson, Mississippi.

Even as SCLC members were discussing Rustin's memo, Local 1733 of the American Federation of State, County and Municipal Employees set a strike for February 12, Abraham Lincoln's birthday. Ninety-five percent of the union membership was black. The wages were low. At the top of the scale a man might get $1.80 an hour, but most earned only a dime above the minimum wage, $1.60 an hour. The white garbage collectors secured the promotions, but above all, Local 1733 sought recognition and bargaining power.

When the strike really began, Mayor Henry Loeb—elected despite the refusal of the black people, 40 percent of the population, to vote for him—declared it illegal. The local NAACP and most of the Negro clergymen and the black population sprang to the support of the garbagemen. (Crises in black communities these days seem to unite Negroes more and more firmly together, throughout all classes.) And union support was gathering in the North, testimony to the failure of unionism itself to solve the problem of racism among its members.

On February 23, King, who by now was in a frenzy with organizing the PPM, jetting here and there across the country to speak and raise funds, and even flying to Switzerland, went to New York to deliver the Centennial Address honoring the one-hundredth birthday of the late W. E. B. DuBois. DuBois, who was almost a man alone in his time and who is currently being rediscovered for about the tenth time, correctly identified "the color line" as the major problem of the twentieth century. (Yet, for all the fire, intelligence, brilliance which he displayed all his life, his close friend, William Monroe Trotter, editor of the Boston *Guardian,* broke with DuBois because he felt he was too moderate. Trotter is overdue for rediscovery.)

Like his talk at Riverside Church, King's address revealed a firm although seldom seen grasp of time and history. He touched on the American fear of Communism and Vietnam; surprisingly he displayed a not unwelcome familiarity with artists-political activists, such as Sean O'Casey and Pablo Neruda.

He then left for Detroit and Newark, planning to be in Memphis for a giant march scheduled for March 28; he had been asked to come by an SCLC affiliate, the Reverend James Lawson. Martin King was a very tired and shaken man. Violence erupted on the march. It shouldn't have disturbed King, given the temper of the times, but it did. It was apparent that neither the SCLC people or the NAACP people had had any success in channeling the black anger into what they called the more creative areas. Black people were seething in Memphis, and King was to say that—having no part in the planning of the march there, and believing that nonviolence was the philosophy under which it would be conducted—he was "caught in a miscalculation." Determined to run things more tightly, King flew to Atlanta for staff conferences.

William Robert Miller in *Martin Luther King Jr.* (Weybright and Talley, 1968) describes the staff meeting. King complained that his aides weren't functioning efficiently and that before the PPM in Washington, "something has to happen within this staff." This would support the observations Tom Kahn makes in *Commentary,* September, 1968, about staff bickering, and also what Bayard Rustin told me about it. But the staff concluded that same night that it was vitally necessary for King to go on with the Washington march after leaving Memphis.

Most of April 4, 1968, in Memphis, King had staff meetings. He spoke of nonviolence, the efficacy and the beauty of it; he spoke with some degree of desperation—he had been speaking of death, his death, and the mountaintop; of the violence that was ripping through Memphis and how it was chipping away at the nonviolent postures of his people, and he was worried.

But his worry slipped away with the approach of dinner time; he and Abernathy were to eat at the home of Reverend and Mrs. Samuel Kyles. King wonder if Mrs. Kyles was a good cook, good enough to fill her table with the best of soul food. Then on his balcony, while waiting for Abernathy to put the finishing touches to his toilet, King spotted a musician he knew and asked him to play a favorite number at the mass meeting scheduled for later that evening. The musician agreed.

King straightened up; the wine (dinner) was all set; Ben Branch had agreed to provide the song and . . . !

Part Two

THE PRIVATE MAN

Twelve

MARTIN King really, really got under my skin. It happened this way:

In his middle teens my eldest son, Gregory, announced in a long letter that he hoped to become a minister. Martin King was the major influence, although Greg later said this was not so. I watched Greg involve himself neck-deep in (Baptist) church activities. When he entered college, he majored in religion and philosophy. But over the years I was pleased to note that he was, to some extent, backing away from his hard position on becoming a theologian, the profession King once hoped to be a part of. Greg's adopted policy of nonviolence underwent a metamorphosis that in many ways reflected the change in millions of black young people; nonviolence slid away from him and I watched with relief. He had to discover things for himself, with some aid from me.

Now Greg is a schoolteacher, and one could claim that the difference between teaching and preaching isn't too great. His brother, Dennis, three years younger, grew up smack into the onrushing tide of young, black radicalism, and looked forward to going to Cornell. Religion, or being religious, has never bothered him.

Among young whites, too, the emphasis on making one's self vulnerable to religious influences is on the wane, mostly among Catholics. But the United States still leads the West in church-goers: 43 of every 100 people. In 1958—a peak year for church attendance—49 out of every 100 persons went. From that point on, attendance dropped off steadily, matching year by year the rising national tensions created by the civil rights movement, when so many churches were asked to open their doors to blacks. Most—North and South—did not. Their reasons were the same, but their methods for keeping blacks out differed. The end result was uniform. As far as the young are concerned, the church had had its chance and blew it. And not only the young, not only the black.

But what else had been expected? On the face of it religions in the West have been and remain pillars of the various economic establishments—monarchies, democracies, and dictatorships. Religions have never met the crying moral needs of man in this century, or truly, in any other.

Western civilization is based on money, not morality, and the concept that in the United States (and a few other countries) the church is separate and distinct from the state is fallacious. When one talks of the exercise of white power in America, one means to an extremely large extent, the exercise of religious power which is also social, political, and economical.

Early on, Martin King expressed disappointment with the white church in its failure to participate to any appreciable degree in the Montgomery boycott. He was to express that disappointment so often that it almost became a whine, a childish petulance, as though he hoped that some God-given miracle *would* make the church the shrine of good he had been raised to think it was. But in his *Letter from Birmingham Jail*, Martin King was in the process of struggling with himself, making himself accept that the church was as he finally *saw* it—real, hard, and with priceless vested interests in maintaining the racial status quo. By 1966, he could say that during his Chicago campaign he had made one all-important mistake: "I underestimated the depths of hate in America."

The truth of the matter is that he had *always* underestimated it. When the hatred became so intense as to kill people, black and white alike, King saw it as a mistake, as aberrant behavior, when in reality the end result of hatred *is* to destroy, to kill.

Much of that hate has been engendered by the church in America. The chorales of the new ecumenicism may fill the air, but there still remains the Protestant, the Catholic, the Jew, the Moslem, the Hindu, the this and the that.

In the United States there are three major and politically, not to mention economically, powerful religious groups. They are the Protestants, the Catholics, and the Jews, and Martin King had to battle all three. They each profess a love of their fellowmen, a subservience to the laws of earthbound governments only so long as their edicts do not conflict with the laws of God. Each abhors, at least in their public statements (Father Coughlin to the contrary), the inequities suffered by their fellow citizens. Each proclaims that one of its major functions is to root out inequality before God and destroy it.

Each group has a positive ethnic composition, with many internal variations, but in the United States the universal cement has been whiteness. None have been greatly disturbed by the presence of segregated churchs. Black Christians have their thing, black Jews have theirs. But it was religious segregation that produced a Martin Luther King, Jr. He was the inevitability of Christianity; he had to come, it was in the cards, just as the time came when black baseball players would become an embarrassment to most white ballplayers, even though for a long time they played in segregated leagues. King was that person who came along to point out that most people who consider themselves Christians were, in fact, something far different from the ideal Christians he envisioned.

The morality of the churches in America has since their establishment been in question by black people. With the advent of slavery in the Western hemisphere, it was no longer a question of morality, for morality had become a rare thing here.

Slavery and the slave trade benefited a lot of people, businesses and governments alike; people most distantly placed from it profited by it. The great churches of Europe with their political, social, and economic connections, directly and indirectly were recharged through the black gold of slavery.

The church was never designed to benefit the beings from whom it derived profit, the slaves. First, introducing slaves to the gospel and, later, allowing them to hold services, diminished the slaveholder's guilt, at least on a superficial level. Second, in teaching about a white Jesus Christ (and downgrading their black gods) who would reward them in heaven, not on earth, the Christian slaveholder was trying to purchase for himself a degree of tranquility and insurance in the midst of a people who were forever to be watched, lest they, in savage retribution for their condition, take his life and destroy the system that had in the first place allowed him to buy, breed, work, and sell another man, who happened to be black.

In the Northern states some Negroes were allowed to become members of some white churches. A few, like the Revolutionary War veteran, Lemuel Haynes and also Richard Allen, even preached in them in the eighteenth century. Allen, inevitably, was beaten in and driven from a white church and later fouded the African Methodist Episcopal Church which today has a million and a quarter members. Black ministers (and worshipers) in the white churches were looked upon as freaks. Because Negro parishioners were segregated in church, and because they could not realistically aspire to positions of power within them, they formed their own. Surely, Martin King, looking out upon the all-black (or nearly so) audiences in Dexter or in his father's church in Atlanta, could not help but know emotionally, even if he could not allow it to penetrate intellectually, that Christianity was at the least a very peculiar religious philosophy. Black churches in the South were constant reminders of the profound failure of Christianity; there the churches were founded in the eighteenth century, the first being built in Petersburg, Virginia, in 1776.

In the North they only came into being in the early nineteenth century.

While virulent racism created the atmosphere for the black church, a willingness to play the game lay behind their actual "success." "The Man" wanted black people to be God-fearing. Well, all right; we will become God-fearing.

Black people hoped that surface compliance would get the white man off their backs. It didn't, but it is historical fact that slave owners felt they had less to fear from slaves who believed in the white man's god than from those who did not. Paradoxically, religion, the white man's religion, played an important part in the lives of Nat Turner and Harriet Tubman and John Brown. They—to the white man's distress— somehow forgot the rules of the game. But the overwhelming majority of black people in slavery played the game all too well, and the white man's religion gradually became an integral part of a warped black reality.

King was a product of the unholy pact the American church made with racism, and when he turned to the church, he turned without demand, resting his case on the Judeo-Christian ethic, not understanding that here he faced the core of American power, for a church-goer is many other things than a mere parishioner. Some survey, however brief, of the major religious groups and their attitudes toward King and the movement is necessary to understand how the power was arrayed against this black preacher, son of a preacher and grandson of a preacher, if we are to understand his failure— and King's failure was massive—to move them to the side of his cause.

First, the Catholics, for upon them must fall the responsibility for the commencement of the slave trade in Africa and black chattel slavery in the New World. They were the first Christians; the Protestants followed soon enough.

From the beginning Catholicism has had an exploitative and dehumanizing relationship to black people. Priests went on the journeys to Africa and there, waiting beside the sandy, windswept barracoons of Badagry in Nigeria and Cape Coast in Ghana, blessed the slaves bound in chains for the New World.

In Santo Domingo (one half of which is now Haiti) Father Bartolomé de Las Casas saw the local Indians enslaved to help "develop" the missions, dying from overwork and starvation. Las Casas pleaded with his superior, Cardinal Ximenes, to replace the Indians with the hardier Africans. But Ximenes reasoned that, since the Africans were a strong and durable people, they would breed quickly, and before long would outnumber their Spanish masters and rebel. Numerous slave revolts in the Spanish colonies and elsewhere proved his estimate to be accurate, for he was overruled by King Carlos V, grandson of Ferdinand and Isabella, who for a time was also Holy Roman Emperor. It was young Carlos who, with some questionable consistency, drove Martin Luther from the church in 1521, and who gave the orders opening the door to the slave trade.

As a result, much, if not all the New World wealth, was Catholic wealth. And since Carlos gave domains to good and loyal Catholics as King of Spain and Holy Roman Emperor, the Church expected to be, and was, handsomely rewarded.

Black people would do well to remember the historical participation of the Catholics in their dehumanization, and only cease to remember when Catholics have undone what they began. (However, there are signs that Negroes have already forgotten: In New York City alone, black Catholics have increased over the past thirty-five years from 7 to above 22 percent. That increase has been for status reasons mainly.)

In *Stride,* King wrote: "One of the glories of the Montgomery movement was that Baptists, Methodists, Lutherans, Presbyterians, Episcopalians and others came together with a willingness to transcend denominational lines. Although no Catholic priests were actively involved in the protest, many of their parishioners took part."

The Montgomery boycott came before the ecumenical mood evoked by Pope John, and that may have been one of the reasons why there was so little participation by priests. Archdiocesan orders against it may have been another. For the Holy Roman Catholic Church will have, will insist, on one thing when it allows its priests and laymen to become involved in secular endeavors: the right to veto those endeavors at its discretion.

Just as black people began to move in the first half of the sixties in their drive for civil rights under liberal Presidents and their administrations, so too did priests tend to become involved in the movement under Pope John and later Pope Paul. Some of them outstripped in their ardor and determination the most fiery blacks in the movement. Father James Groppi of Milwaukee, for example, said: "I don't know that a nonviolent revolution is, in fact, realistic in the United States. ... Anyway, the whole problem of racism boils down to this: If the Church was really doing its job, the phenomenon of racism would have disappeared a long time ago."

Warren Hinckle, a former *Ramparts* editor (*Ramparts* in its early days was a "radical" Catholic publication), contends that the job the Church was doing, led by its liberals who "were at best careful progressives," was to adapt "reasonably to the times."

Brother Brightness is positive that the Church did not make even that minimum effort, pointing out that for twelve years the American Consistory had nothing on its agenda pertinent to civil rights. Brother Brightness—that is the name I've given him—is an ex-Jesuit. I found it difficult to find ranking Catholic churchmen who would talk to me about Martin King. I met Brother Brightness on a beach in St. Thomas two years ago. Today he is actively engaged in civil rights.

There was no basic Catholic adaptation to King or the movement. "The Catholic power structure hated King," Brother Brightness told me. We spent several afternoons taping interviews and going over material he'd brought for my research. "Sometimes it forbade the people and the priests to become involved with him. There were times when they faced minor laymen's revolts. In such cases, it was simple enough for the structure to beat the people to participation in that particular effort of King's, thus effectively maintaining control over them."

Large, large numbers of Catholics participated in the 1963 March on Washington, and there on the program was Archbishop O'Boyle, who demonstrated that he would use his veto if John Lewis did not change his speech. O'Boyle would shatter the portrait of unity by withdrawing from the program.

Brother Brightness, his voice rushing forth from the tape, says: "Did you know that Catholics were not even allowed to attend the services held by King?"

"No."

"Not only was he black, you know, but a Protestant, the most natural enemy of Catholics."

Is it strange to consider that King's rise not only matched the decline in Catholic church attendance, but the advent of the ecumenical spirit that issued from the Vatican in the early sixties?

But late, very late in King's life, under date of November 1, 1967, came a letter by the Very Reverend Pedro Arrupe, S.J., General of the Society of Jesus, on *The Interracial Apostolate*. It was addressed to Fathers, Scholastics, and Brothers of the American Assistancy. Note that the letter came on the downside of the movement, after Birmingham, St. Augustine, Chicago, Selma, after the rise of black radicalism. General Arrupe wrote:

> The gravity of the current racial crisis in the United States and its serious impact upon Christian doctrine and practice impel me to address this letter to you. I do so with a great sense of responsibility and after consultation with the American Provincials and other men knowledgeable in the field of race relations. . . .

The racial crisis involves, before all else, a direct challenge to our sincerity in professing a Christian concept of man. . . . Pope Paul VI, on October 29, 1967, stated, "The Second Vatican Council clearly and repeatedly condemned racism in its various forms as being an offense against human dignity. . . ." It is chastening to recall that, before the Civil War, some American Jesuit houses owned Negro slaves. It is humbling to remember that, until recently, a number of Jesuit institutions did not admit qualified Negroes, even in areas where civil restrictions against integrated schools did not prevail, and this even in the case of Catholic Negroes. It is embarrassing to note that, up to the present, some of our institutions have effected what seems to be little more than token integration of the Negro.

One of those discriminating institutions was Georgetown University in Washington, D.C., a Jesuit institution, which was built by slaves owned by the society. The second president of this oldest Catholic university in the nation, oddly enough, was a black man (or partly black, but in the United States that means *all* black), Father Patrick Francis Healy, S.J., Ph.D.; he was appointed July 31, 1874. A brother, James Augustine Healy, was made Bishop of Portland, Maine, in 1875; this Healy was instrumental in beating down the attempts of Protestants to levy taxes on Catholic churches and institutions. A third brother, Alexander Sherwood Healy, was rector of Boston Cathedral, appointed in 1870.

When I told Brother Brightness about the Healys, he exclaimed, "That Healy of Georgtown. I've seen his picture many times, *but he does not look black,* and no one ever went out of his way to tell others that he was."

The Healys came along at a time when great masses of Catholics seized mightily on the American dream and in some cases were willing to share it with others in order to make it more attainable for themselves. (Those days have passed, but for some blacks, the illusion persists. For example, the *apparent* clerical support of the movement was reflected in a

1963 *Newsweek* poll: 58 percent of the Negroes questioned thought priests were helpful in their cause.) Warren Hinckle comments on the period when the Healys were acceptable: "In the late nineteenth century, a distinct liberal Catholicism began to emerge in America. . . . Fearful that sly Protestant insinuations that Catholics would obey Rome before Washington would curtail the Church's growing acceptance and affluence, they recognized the need to somehow square the authoritarian tradition of the Church with the country's democratic principles."

The result: the Healy brothers, offsprings of a white father and black mother. They were, it seems, the token high-ranking blacks in the United States Church hierarchy. *Today, of 56,000 priests, only 170 are black* and one half of those belong to the Black Catholic Clergy Caucus. These thin numbers did not aid King, simply because they could not, in any appreciable way, and in Chicago, King found himself face to face with Polish Catholics in the main, who were ready to tear him limb from limb as he led marches through their neighborhoods. But they, of all white Catholics, were trying hardest to prove that they were the equals of other white Catholics, which they were not.

Brother Brightness: "You just can't get any lower than a Polish Catholic. They are Yanko—nonwhite, a mere notch above black Catholics, and Irish and Latin Catholics look down on them."

With such ethnic fragmentation within the Church, it is no wonder that Catholics easily fall prey to racism. And King stood for everything the Church was firmly opposed to. For one thing, the thrust of his movement was positively toward complete and unequivocal equality. As the Church is now constituted, there can be no such thing. The Catholic Church is, according to Ferdinand Lundberg (*The Rich and the Super-Rich*, Lyle Stuart, 1968), "the leading property-holding church, although most Catholics are quite poor." King's demand late in his career for a guaranteed annual income, flew in the face of a church tradition, the corporate gathering of wealth.

Also, King's commitment to help end the war in Vietnam was at the other end of the Catholic position. The New York *Times,* February 15, 1966, in observing that most churches were against the war, went on to say that, "The main exception to the general trend, of course, is the American hierarchy of the Roman Catholic Church, which has largely been silent, or as in the case of several leaders such as Cardinal Spellman of New York, supported the war effort. The position of the American Catholic hierarchy, however, contratsts sharply with the peace efforts of Pope Paul."

King and Abernathy had had an audience with Pope Paul back in 1964, and King said, "The Pope made it palpably clear that he is a friend of the Negro people, and asked me to tell the American Negroes that he is committed to the cause of civil rights in the United States."

It is clear that what Pope Paul said in 1964 and what the ranking Catholics in this nation say today, are two vastly different things. King misled the Pope somewhat by reporting that the Civil Rights Act of 1964 was being implemented in the South. He expressed surprise at "the degree of compliance in Southern communities."

But, to return to 1966, the year of black power, of King's hardening stand of no more war in Vietnam, of demands for improving the condition of the nation's poor, demands that smacked of no religious philosophy—that was the year the Catholics came out swinging.

Brother Brightness reported: "There was a great deal of talk among the Irish community about King's 'indiscretions,' mostly by an FBI agent named K——, a cousin of mine. I've never met him. He passed through the whole of Pennsylvania, although he was stationed in New York at the time. This would be back in '66. He talked about King's 'indiscretions' with women; that he had a chick in every town. I got that from about forty Irish Catholics, all over the state. And it came from one man. But I can't imagine why, if he were assigned to New York, he would be going around in Pennsylvania, can you?"

I said, "Maybe that was his new assignment."

"Hey! Well, if K—— had this information, then the bishops in this country had it. I'm sure it's viable to say that his first loyalties were to the bishops and then to America."

Thirteen

CRITICAL examination proves that "there are precious few Negro-Jewish relations in the United States today." Will Maslow, President of the American Jewish Congress, made that statement in a *Midstream* (December, 1966) symposium on black anti-Semitism. This is a truth that has been obscured by the Jewish leadership, which has been, it now appears, leading an army without soldiers. While it seems to be dedicated to "translating democratic ideals into a way of life for all Americans in our time," as the slogan of the Anti-Defamation League of B'nai B'rith states, the average Jew regards the black man pretty much in the same way as the average Catholic or Protestant. The Jewish man in the street, however, unlike the rank-and-file Catholic or Protestant, was perfectly content to let Jewish leadership create the illusion that all Jews were in accord in feeling a sense of closeness to Negroes.

The fact of the matter is that Jewish interest in black problems is comparatively recent. Doubtless, the near virulence of American anti-Semitism, that is, white anti-Semitism, played a vital role in that interest. Thus there appeared to be a firm liaison between Jew and black because of the similarity of their aspirations. Both groups wished to reach a status where each could enjoy the rights held by nonblack and non-Jewish citizens. The fact that both Jews and blacks were set together or, at least, within hailing distance of one another in the poverty box, helped solidify this liaison even in illusion, and

I must point out that sometimes it was not illusory. The two communities enjoyed a sort of symbiosis of the mutually oppressed. At the bottom of the ladder black and Jew could prey on each other; there they could live in America without disturbing the white, Anglo-Saxon Protestant power structure which was in the process of accepting honorary memberships from the Catholics.

Yet in spite of virulent anti-Semitism in the Western world, the bulk of the Jewish population in America was evolving, often within a single generation, from an immigrant poor group to middle-class status, and in the process accruing a power that would become effective socially, academically, politically, and economically.

But no matter how secure his position appeared to be, the Jew has had to walk a narrow line, forever watching his flanks, while nudging his way into arenas where he could fully exercise his new power. That he *could* exercise power at all often made him lose sight of the sources of real power—numbers. Power always evolves from numbers of people, numbers of dollars, numbers of friends. While he had sight of that truth, the Jew must have observed that, if Anglo-Saxon America, with its ethnic auxiliaries of lesser backgrounds, decided to rid itself of troublesome minorities, those that insisted on certain rights and opportunities that could only come at the expense of others (which was precisely the way the others got theirs), it would have to begin with that largest, most troublesome, most guilt-provoking minority, the American Negro.

That a Gentile majority could first consider the exploitation and possible elimination of a minority that was *not* Jewish, was a luxury Jews had never enjoyed anywhere else in this world. *They* had been the immediate targets for exploitation; *they* endured the pogroms, *they* had been the victims of bigots and political hustlers; *they* were forever the scapegoats. It followed then that as long as the blacks were safe, they were safe, and it became inevitable that the interests of the Negro, mainly survival, coincided temporarily with the interests of the Jew, at least in the area defined by Jewish leaders as humanitarianism.

Martin King's humanitarianism appealed immensely to U.S. Jews.* My friend, Person A, told me that, "No sooner did King appear on the verge of becoming a national figure, than a couple of Jews were at him, one on each ear." Person A is Jewish. He told me this with humorous pride, saying, in so many words, that a Jew knows a good thing when he sees it. There was no reason for Jews not to have been at King's side. After all, through the American Jewish Committee they had helped Dr. Kenneth Clark prepare the material that helped to bring about the Supreme Court decision of 1954. Jewish attorneys long have been associated with the Legal Defense Fund of the NAACP. Again, I am talking about leadership. This comradeship did not extend from top to bottom.

Morris Abram, former president of Brandeis University, told me something of Jews and Martin King: "All during the years that I lived in the South, critical years, there was a lot of harassment of anyone who wanted to deviate from the status quo. . . . Jews were pretty much like everyone else in their *public* manifestations. They were different in their private thoughts.

"It is true that many of them were frightened to death by virtue of the fact that Martin and the whole movement was surfacing issues that would have been easier to live with if they were not surfaced. But . . . it was recognized that—two things: he was right, and that he indeed was a force of reason in this revolution and that *his aspirations were those which society could easily accommodate without any difficulty.* [Italics added.]

"Yet, when I was President of the American Jewish Committee, and we decided to give him the National Committee's

* King was a welcome alternative to Malcolm in the Jewish community. Malcolm made many, what most Jews would consider, anti-Semitic statements. In Lagos in 1964, after his break with Elijah Muhammad, he was asked if he was working with Jews, or would he, and he said, "I'm working with white people and Jews are white."

highest award, I had to talk to some of our leaders and explain why it was that I figured that he was one of the greatest living Americans. But it went through and it was a great occasion when he received the American Liberties Medallion. No one ever regretted it. But there was an inertia, a feeling of, well, you know, let well enough alone.

"But I don't really think that you could compare the average Jewish sentiment about Martin with the average white, non-Jewish sentiment. I think the Jewish sentiment was favorable."

There can be no doubt that Jewish sentiment was indeed more favorable than that of white Catholics and Protestants, and Jews backed up their support of King with the money SCLC so desperately needed. Abram: "I would suggest to you that per capita, the support of SCLC was very heavily Jewish, and it was so until the end."

As far as the relationship between King and the Jewish people was concerned, most Protestants and Catholics saw nothing unusual in it; wasn't that the way it had always been? And for many of them it was the proof they were seeking that the movement was infiltrated and engineered by Communists. For large numbers of Catholics and Protestants, Jewish was and remains synonymous with Communist. Of course this is a way of remaining anti-Semitic, but concealing it behind a political rather than racial mask.

What happened to the black and Jew to dissolve their tenuous relationship is a matter of record. Blacks demanded black leadership; that meant Jews had to leave many of the offices they held in civil rights organizations. The New York City school strike of 1968, which developed into a racial crisis between mostly Jewish teachers and black parents, further widened the gulf between the two groups.

The novelist, Chester Himes, who is himself part Jewish, made this observation: "It was obvious, even when I was a little boy, you know, in the South, that the only stores black people could go into were owned by Jews. The Jew has always taken the black man as a market. The Jews found out that in a basically anti-Semitic country like America, the most available market for a poor Jew on the lower rung of business, was the black man. That was his market. He could rent them houses and he could sell them food. Well, then they abused the black man."

But exploitation of the blacks by Jews was not to be discussed openly until the fifties and sixties and then analysis of the nature of the relationship led straight to a real schism between the two groups. Oddly enough, the Jews first attacked the blacks. The attack was launched in New York's intellectual community by Norman Podhoretz's article, "My Negro Problem and Ours" which was published in *Commentary* (February, 1963) the magazine of which he is editor. The two subsequent issues of the magazine contained many indignant letters by blacks and Jews, most of which denied or tried to explain away black anti-Semitism.

Now that it was in the open, Jews took off in full cry, howling down any display of black anti-Semitism. They felt that, having contributed so heavily to black causes, they did not deserve such treatment from the blacks. They pointed out that they had always been in the forefront of the fight for civil rights, and that Goodman and Schwerner had died for the movement. Former New York City Human Rights Commissioner, William Booth, said, however, that "Some Jews have been in the forefront, it is true, but many others have not."

Under pressure from the New York Board of Rabbis for not responding to what they called the growth of anti-Semitic demonstrations in the city, Booth was given a judgeship. Mayor Lindsay denied that he was replaced under pressure, but the move soured Negroes both on Lindsay and on this display of Jewish power. (Booth is reported to have told several people that he was indeed fired.)

In the middle sixties the issue blew wide open at a CORE meeting in Westchester County. The most widely circulated account had it that a local CORE leader shouted that Hitler had been right to do what he did to the Jews. But the other side of the account got little circulation. It seems that the black man was angrily responding to a racial insult by a Jew.

A 1965 study by the Anti-Defamation League revealed that Negroes held Jews in higher esteem than they did other whites. This and other information designed to show that the cry of black anti-Semitism was in fact not altogether valid, was disputed by the Jewish community. The teachers' strike in New York split the two communities right down the middle. During the strike I had a long conversation with an official at the American Jewish Committee, and he told me that AJC was investigating the possibility that influences outside the black and Jewish communities were involved in creating and maintaining hostility between them.

Not only was there a split between the two communities, there was a growing gap between the Jewish parent and youngster. Many of the kids told me that they felt that on the issue of race, their parents were steadily sidling toward the positions of other white groups, abandoning the liberal positions they once had so proudly and publicly held.

Jewish contributions to CORE and SNCC all but dried up after the advent of black power, and were channeled instead to SCLC. Martin King would respond to this aid. And he did. On December 11, 1966, King spoke from Atlanta over a nation-wide telephone hook-up sponsored by the American Jewish Conference on Soviet Jewry. Asking a black man to plead the case of their brothers in Russia sharply recalled the handicaps both peoples lived under. In part King said that day:

"While Jews in Russia may not be physically murdered as they were in Nazi Germany, they are facing every day a kind of spiritual and cultural genocide. Individual Jews may in the main be physically and economically secure in Russia, but the absence of opportunity to associate as Jews in the enjoyment of Jewish culture and religious experience becomes a severe limitation upon the individual ... *When you are written out of history as a people, when you are given no choice but to accept the majority culture, you are denied an aspect of your own destiny. Ultimately you suffer a corrosion of your self-understanding and your self-respect."* [Italics added.]

Morris Abram assessed the value of King's address:

"I've been involved in the whole Russian Jewry problem as the U.S. Representative to the Human Rights Commission of the United States. They [the Soviets] react very strongly, vociferously to this charge [of anti-Semitism].

"And there's no doubt that Martin with his stand on Vietnam, what it was, with his stand on human rights, what it was, as a black man whom they could scarcely accuse of imperialism and colonialism, it had a deep effect; it cut them. I think his voice wave very useful in this cause."

It was not, however, useful in mending the rift between black and Jew, for black power, born in the summer of that year, had shifted attention from King to Stokley Carmichael; indeed, the militants were denouncing nonviolence with every breath, and as far as they were concerned, the white power structure included Jews.

Jewish leadership seemed to have run out of black allies; there was King, of course, and Bayard Rustin. Roy Wilkins could be counted on, and A. Philip Randolph and Whitney Young, Jr. But King possessed the stature. So, when the New Politics Convention convened in Chicago in late summer of 1967 and some of the black delegates sought a condemnation of Israel for annexing Arab territories during the Six-Day War, Morris B. Abram and the American Jewish Committee hurried to King (who had made the convention's opening address) to request that he refute the stand taken by the black caucus on Israel. That request was not unlike a demand. And King responded, although it was clear to many observers at the time that there was no healing the split between groups like CORE and SNCC and SCLC. The fact that some of SCLC's younger staff members attended the convention only underscores even further the differences between the radicals of SCLC and the older staffers.

In a letter to Abram, parts of which were incorporated into an AJC press release, King said:

"SCLC has repeatedly stated that the Middle East problem embodies the related questions of security and development. *Israel's right to exist as a State in security is incontestable. At the same time the great powers have the obligation to recognize that the Arab world is in a state of imposed poverty and backwardness that must threaten peace and harmony.* Until a concerted and democratic program of assistance is affected, tensions cannot be relieved. Neither Israel nor its neighbors can live in peace without an underlying basis of economic and social development.

"At the heart of the problem are oil interests."

And, writing of SCLC's role at the convention, King went on:

"Serious distortions by the press have created an impression that SCLC was a part of the group at the Chicago Conference of New Politics. . . . The facts are as follows: The staff members of SCLC who attended the conference (not as official delegates) were the most vigorous and articulate opponents of the simplistic resolution on the Middle East question. As a result of this opposition, the black caucus modified its stand and the convention voted to eliminate references to Zionism. . . . This change was the direct result of the spirited opposition on the floor by Hosea Williams."

The body of King's letter was given over to his views on black anti-Semitism. Certainly the telegrams that followed AJC's request for a refutation of the black caucas were enough to anger anyone. They came from not only Abram, but Jordan Brand, NCRAC chairman; Dr. Maurice Eisendrath, President, Union of American Hebrew Congregations; Adolph Held, President, Jewish Labor Committee; Joseph Karasick, President, Union of Orthodox Jewish Congregations of America; Rabbi Arthur J. Lelyveld, President, American Jewish Congress; Henry N. Rapaport, President, United Synagogue of America; Samuel Samuels, National Commander, Jewish War

Veterans; Dore Schary, National Chairman, Anti-Defamation League of B'nai B'rith and Mrs. Leonard Weiner, President, National Council of Jewish Women.

The joint telegram read:

To: Rev. Martin Luther King

"Our organizations share a deep commitment to full equality in an integrated, plural society. We believe that its attainment demands action by a coalition of groups for accelerated and dramatic social change. We have admired and respected your advocacy of these goals and your leadership over the years.

"Now we are profoundly distressed by the recent New Politics Conventions. The apartheid of the adopted structure and the lack of democratic procedure; the absence of any specific constructive program for the advancement of equal opportunity; the anti-Semitism in spite of disavowals; the irrational anti-Israel resolution; all are disturbing and destructive. We believe that they also are antithetical to everything you have stood for.

"Because of your presence at the Convention, and the presence of your name on the National Council of the Conference for New Politics, we fear that these destructive positions may gain a show of respectability. We urge you to disassociate yourself publicly from the malevolence which found expression in the resolutions of the New Politics Convention."

King's response is worth repeating:

"The question that troubles many Jews and other concerned Americans is why oppressed Negroes should harbor any anti-Semitism at all. Prejudice and discrimination can only harm them; therefore it would appear that they should be virtually immune to their sinister appeal.

"The limited degree of Negro anti-Semitism is substantially a Northern ghetto phenomenon; it virtually does not exist in the South. The urban Negro has a special and unique relationship to Jews. On the one hand, he is associated with Jews as some of his most committed and generous partners in the civil rights struggle. On the other hand, he meets them daily as slum landlords and gouging shopkeepers. Jews have identified with Negroes voluntarily in the freedom movement, motivated by their religious and cultural commitment to justice. The other Jews who are engaged in commerce in the ghettos are remnants of older communities. A great many Negro ghettos were formerly Jewish neighborhoods; some shopkeepers and landlords remained as population changes occurred. They operate with the ethics of marginal business entrepreneurs, not Jewish ethics, but the distinction is lost on some Negroes who are maltreated by them. Such Negroes, caught in frustration and irrational anger, parrot racial epithets. They foolishly add to the social poison that injures themselves and their own people.

"It would be a tragic and immoral mistake to identify the mass of Negroes with the very small number that succumb to cheap and dishonest slogans, just as it would be a serious error to identify all Jews with the few who exploit Negroes under their economic sway.

"Negroes cannot rationally expect honorable Jews to curb the few who are racious (*sic*); they have no means of disciplining or suppressing them. We can only expect them to share our disgust and disdain. Negroes cannot be expected to curb and eliminate the few who are anti-Semitic, because they are subject to no controls we can exercise. We can, however, oppose them and have, in concrete ways. . . ."

Almost exactly one year later, King dead and Morris Abram installed as the new president of Brandeis University, Coretta Scott King took up where her late husband had left off. At Abram's inauguration she said of the issue of black and Jewish differences: "What is needed is for both groups to face boldly the sharpening confrontation and for each to be honest to the other in acknowledging the conflict. . . . Finally, it must be said that there is a mutual dependence. The Negro struggle has been aided by the long Jewish fight for equality. In the same sense the Negro revolution has incontestably enlarged tolerance and understanding not only for black people, but for all minorities. It is not coincidence that the sharpest drop in anti-Semitism has occurred in the period of the Negro revolt. It was inevitable that as our fight stimulated the conscience of the nation, it benefited Jewish relations with the larger community."

That may prove to be the ultimate measure of the relationship between King and Jewish Americans, but it is clear that they could and did exercise power as far as King was concerned. In the matter of the New Politics Convention, Jewish leaders utilized King as the "house Negro" to refute the allegations of other more militant Negroes. The large number of Jewish organizations signing the telegram to King cannot be described as anything other than a thinly veiled threat, most probably to withhold financial support from SCLC.

Most power—economic, political, and social—resides chiefly in the hands of the Protestants. They control government, the corporations, the destiny of this land and its peoples. Like Catholicism, Protestantism held a vested interest in the slave trade and slavery, and indeed, Professor C. L. R. James has long contended that the industrial revolutions of Europe as well as America, were founded on the sale and labor of black men, women, and children.

The largest number of Protestants in America believe in the fundamental teachings of the Bible, finding in that collection of legends, tales, laws, and inspirations, ample precedents for maintaining racial segregation. We have seen how racism within the church forced the founding of black churches. Racism was the cause of the formation of the Southern Baptist Convention in 1845, which broke away from the national organization because Northern Baptists were in some cases opposed to slavery. There are almost no black members in the SBC.

Although King was a Baptist, his favorite teacher, Dr. Harold DeWolf, is a Methodist. I interviewed Dr. DeWolf in his office at American University in Washington, where he is a dean of the theology department. He is a small, soft-spoken man, neatly tailored, and he struck me as being more a businessman than a theologian.

He spoke highly of King and is called Uncle Harold by King's children. We did the interview in late afternoon, the autumn shadows growing long outside his window. It became clear that Dr. DeWolf (and he said it was true) and King had had some differences of a philosophical nature. For example, before King mounted the Poor People's March, he had spoken about the need to hold massive civil disobedience demonstrations around the country, so massive that they could tie up whole cities. Said DeWolf: "I would not have supported the massive displays of civil disobedience in the large cities that Martin was planning."

During the course of the interview, DeWolf mentioned Rhodesia where his son lives, expecting to be thrown out any time. Indeed, he may have been sent out since I talked to his father. DeWolf spoke of his visits there and said: "In Rhodesia I would tell them [the Africans] about King. I would tell them about his nonviolent philosophy and they would shrug their shoulders and say, 'Well, of course the Negroes are only one-tenth of the people and we suppose they have to be that way. But we don't think that's the way in Africa. We think we ought to rise up here with guns and take it over.' But I told them they had the numbers to make nonviolence work, and recommended a general strike that could topple the government in Rhodesia in forty-eight hours."

I glanced down at the tape recorder, then out the window, DeWolf's words echoing in my mind. I felt then, as I have felt many times, helpless in the face of such patronizing religiosity. And I would have questioned him about the two statements, but I was not there to run a debate, merely to listen and to interpret, to put together the pieces of King's life. Harold DeWolf was an important piece, a mentor, examiner, judge.

For it was clear that afternoon that what DeWolf approved of and recommended to Africans was precisely what he disapproved of, would not recommend and opposed, for American blacks, both groups similarly oppressed. Obviously, save for his son and daughter-in-law, he had no interests in Rhodesia. Therefore, a general strike—is such a tactic different from massive displays of civil disobedience?—was all right for that country. In the United States where his roots must go deep in terms of family, career, and profession, the same tactic proposed for blacks made his hackles rise.

But then, American missionaries have worked in places like Africa, seeking to Christianize the people, but those same converts visiting the missions' home churches in the United States have been refused entrance. It is to be remembered that the big difference between the Protestants and the Catholics was that the former kicked blacks out of their churches. The Catholics never dismissed nonwhites to operate on their own, choosing rather to guide, expose the heathen to God, receive their labors, and convert them into corporate wealth.

Left to their own devices by the Protestants, the black churches flourished, for most Negroes are of course Protestant. Nearly all are located in the inner cities, and some of them, like Friendship Baptist Church in New York, have even been cited as slumlords. Black churches have been granted tax-exempt status, and they are as eager to raise money and keep it as any white church. In New York black churches own between $70,000,000 and $100,000,000 worth of property; white Protestant churches own many, many times that. Many black churches work within larger conferences, but control is autonomous and the churches often family owned.

The National Council of Churches, which represents most major Protestant churches in the country, has a constituency of about 42,000,000 people. Of that number, 12,000,000 are black. One million blacks attend churches that are predominantly white. (The black Catholic constituency in the United States is about 600,000 people. There is one black bishop.)

The Protestant establishment has always been slicker than the Catholic; there have been token Negroes in positions with national organizations for a number of years now, but increasingly those blacks have had to move to more militant postures, claiming that, while the positions are theirs, they have little or no authority. The Reverend Robert C. Chapman, an Episcopal staff member of the NCC, said in an interview with the New York *Times* (July 27, 1969) "The fact is that black and white church officials have unequal voices when they speak."

Black clergymen within the structure have reluctantly voiced the opinion that racism in the church is the major factor in the growing division between black and white ministers. The NCC is on record in favor of civil rights, but its officials, and some have stated so, have not yet acted on the advice of the black members of their staffs, have not allowed them to participate in decision making.

The Southern Baptist Convention with its 12,000,000 members has not supported the NCC on civil rights. It is the religious affiliation of the most rabid bigots in America, so it is no wonder. The leaders of the SBC contend that racial matters are political, not religious, and therefore have no place in religious discussions. Thirty percent backed the candidacy of George Wallace in 1968, and 44 percent supported Richard Nixon; 60 percent, it was revealed in a random poll, believed the actions of the United States in Vietnam were the right ones.

King had trouble with white Protestants, but he also had trouble with black ones. The Reverend Dr. Joseph Harrison Jackson, pastor of the Olivet Baptist Church in Chicago, a position he's held for twenty-eight years, led the black anti-King forces. From the beginning of King's career to its tragic end, Dr. Jackson stood opposed to him and to his movement. Jackson, who is quick to praise the conservative right, is equally fast at labeling the left. He is opposed to militancy, to demonstrations, to anything that might disturb the status quo; younger blacks dislike him and have on occasion booed him so thoroughly that he was unable to speak.

Adam Clayton Powell and King were at odds from time to time, too, but they managed to make peace. The difference between Powell and Jackson was that the latter really was a white Negro, completely in the corner of the white power structure, and soon enough replaced King as Lyndon Johnson's "black minister-in-residence" in the White House when King fell from grace. Jackson, it appears, defended racism. Powell on the other hand was simply protecting his position as "king of the hill." He was leading demonstrations in Harlem while King was still in Atlanta University's Laboratory High School. Not only was he "boss" of Harlem by virtue of pastoring its largest Baptist church, but by right of the ballot; he was its Congressional representative.

When Mayor Robert F. Wagner invited King to New York in the wake of the rebellions that occurred there that summer of 1964 when Goodman, Chaney, and Schwerner were found murdered, Powell hit the ceiling. He had not been consulted, and it was *his* district. He made it clear that King was poaching on alien territory. As far as Powell was concerned, King could rule the roost in every section of the country but New York. That was his, and he could not afford to be closely aligned with nonviolence; he'd seldom preached it and, in fact, had often shared the platforms in Harlem Square with Malcolm X and other black nationalists.

Martin King was not an ignorant man. He must have known to some degree all that I've set down here and more. And he did once say that he "had doubts that religion was intellectually responsible." He also must have had doubts that, given its history, the church in America could be swung over to the support—the complete and unequivocal support—of civil rights. Like Don Quixote, he tilted with windmills and he had to lose; there was just too much white power for him to contend with.

And he realized this for, even as he fought futilely to involve the church, he increasingly left it out of his writings, writings edged by his frustration toward a new and escalating militancy. "I am not sad that black Americans are rebelling; this was not only inevitable but eminently desirable."

Still, out of the chaos of the American church crumbling down around him in its total failure to be moved, there were signs that King, nevertheless, had planted seeds that would be tended by others.

It is probable that the last thing James Forman would like to be called is a disciple of King. History may claim so. He was one of the many college-trained young men who, caught up in the first flush of black movement during and after Montgomery, rushed to join SNCC, and although King and his SCLC and SNCC had grave differences, Forman and others like him emerged because there was a time in which a man named Martin King was alive and doing things in the United States.

In the spring of 1969, James Forman, now with gray in his hair and beard, neatly dressed in a suit instead of the usual SNCC overalls, walked into Riverside Church in Manhattan, where King had given his greatest sermon on the war two years before. There, in the company of six other members of the Black Economic Development Conference, he read his "Black Manifesto," calling for the churches and synagogues of America to pay to the BEDC the sum of $500,000,000 (this sum was later raised to $3 billion) for reparations to blacks for their years of slavery and second-class status. The Black Economic Development Conference would use the money to create a land bank in the South, a black university, black publishing house and television facilities.

The Black Manifesto was supported by large numbers of black ministers and priests within the Protestant and Catholic churches. Predictably, the Catholic leadership denounced the manifesto and has refused to accede to any of its demands. The Jewish Defense League, which now stands at least publicly condemned by other Jews, took ads in the New York *Times,* openly threatening to defend synagogues from James Forman's approach.

In September, 1969, the National Council of Churches voted to meet at least part way the demands of the manifesto, by raising $500,000 and later "tens of millions more." In the same month, Dr. Joseph Jackson in Kansas City denounced black militancy and called the Black Manifesto "the same old Red manifesto painted black and an echo of the Communist demands of Karl Marx. . . . The civil rights movement," he went on, "must now modify its course and move in a different direction. It must cease to be a campaign of color. . . ."

There will be no monies coming from the Southern Baptist Convention.

For all the opposition to the Black Manifesto since it was first presented, a lot of thinking has gone on among church leadership, and considerably more action than many observers expected. But the fact remains that Forman came up with a plan that dealt in tangibles—money is a very tangible item. Martin King, on the other hand, urged a moral commitment. But morals are hard to lay hands on, and when a man is told that his morals are in pretty shoddy shape, he becomes incensed, especially if he believes they are all right. Forman simply went out to give people the chance to ease their consciences with money. In part, his direct assault has succeeded, whereas King's tactics never did. Yet from King to Forman there is a positive link—a relationship. Forman may say that King failed when he attacked the power of the churches, but Forman bears outstanding witness to the truth that King was not a complete flop; James Forman makes Martin King look awfully good.

Fourteen

IF King was aware of the power aligned against him in the church, and had had doubts about the intellectual honesty of religion, why then did he become a churchman? Here and there over the years he mentioned that he wished to return to his books, to indulge in scholarship and even to teach at a university.

The events that created King were at fever pitch long, long before he was born, and they were all steeped in racism. Being a black man, there was no escape for King; being of the black middle class, his efforts to find himself were even more complicated than those of the average black man.

There was already a black middle class when the Emancipation Proclamation came in 1863. These were free blacks and most were the products of black and white sexual unions. When all black people were freed, the highest social value among them was color. The more reflected was the white in the black, the more white became the black.

The second highest value was employment. This had had roots in slavery where the house servant was regarded as several cuts above the field hand; and where the artisan, the brickmaker, the carpenter, the blacksmith, were skilled enough to be rented out. Among the emancipated, the further away from the soil a man labored, the higher his status in the black community.

The third value became education. At the end of the Civil War and during Reconstruction, whites, believing that some education would be a good thing for the Freedmen, founded a number of Negro colleges. Few of them were purely academic institutions then. They tended to be vocational, taught skills and crafts. That was the way whites wanted it. They were not altogether sure black people in their new-found freedom were capable of absorbing the glories of Western civilization, why push it? The emphasis on vocational educations was actually a perpetuation of segregation. The nation was exploding beyond the crude stages of the industrial revolution into advanced technology; black people were meant to remain behind. Whites were sure they had done the right thing when, in 1895, Booker T. Washington gave his "Atlanta Compromise" speech asking black people to "cast down" their buckets where they were, and in which he assured the crackers that "In all things that are purely social we can be as separate as the fingers, yet one as the hand in all things essential to mutual progress."

In the same speech Washington had called for an end to discrimination, and sounded a gentle tinkle of alarm at the fantastic influx of European laborers, who were reaping the benefits due the Negro.

But for all their dubious worth, the schools—and Washington headed the most prestigious at this time, Tuskegee Institute—were institutions of, if not higher education, a *different* education than black people had been able to get before, with the exception of a very few.

Thus, for the black middle class, the values were education, employment, and color.

The King family resolutely worked its way into Atlanta's middle class.

Consider employment. Most of King's biographers point with some pride to King's grandfather's plantation-style, field hand status. Martin Luther King, Sr., left his father's farm for the streets of Atlanta where he did the best he could in that urban setting. In short order, he was preaching in two small Baptist churches before he had "paper one." Martin, Sr., had not yet graduated from high school. But, by taking evening classes, he did get his diploma and went on to take classes at Morehouse College.

Adam Daniel Williams had been cut from the same tough cloth before King, Sr., came down the pike. He, too, had taken courses at Morehouse and, more importantly, put Ebenezer Baptist Church back in the black through his judicious administration. King, Sr., married Williams' daughter Alberta. She had gone to Hampton, where Booker T. Washington was teaching at the time. She had also attended Spelman College in Atlanta, and worked briefly as a teacher.

In terms of education, the Kings appear to have come late to it, and to have had spotty contact with it even then, not that it was their fault, but with education being so crucially important in the black Atlanta community, the uneducated or partially educated man found himself held in contempt, especially if he tried to move in circles inhabited by college graduates. Early in his career Martin, Sr., must have carried the odious title of "jackleg" which, among Negroes, means unlettered, untrained but functioning, not always successfully, on sheer nerve.

If the Kings did not quite achieve status through education, they also missed it in terms of color. Rare is the black man who does not have some white blood lurking somewhere in his genes. The Kings had Irish, Indian, and Negro blood, but it appears to have been rather evenly mixed, for the Kings were what black people used to call a "pleasing brown." It has been noted by the legions of students concerned with the Negro in America that black men tend to marry women whose skins are lighter than theirs. Martin, Sr., threw a wrench into the works; Alberta Williams appeared to be a full-blooded Negro, darker in complexion than he was.

The King family came to whatever position of prominence it held in Atlanta insularly, as did almost every other member of the black middle class, rarely coming in contact with the white world even economically. The King income was derived entirely from the black community. That was not bad. Indeed, the community could view with pride the fact that *it* and not whites, was able to provide the funds to maintain the King family in near high fashion.

The late sociologist, E. Franklin Frazier, pointed out in his *Black Bourgeoisie* (The Macmillan Company, 1962) that after World War I the middle-class values began to change; lightness of color, for example, became less important than solid achievements in the professions. But there are still a goodly number of fair-skinned Negroes, older people to be sure, who consider themselves superior to Negroes with darker skins. Black societies in cities like Washington, D.C., and Atlanta, are still touched with the color-bug.

King himself, apparently, had some color hang-up. Over a period of about two years I had a series of running conversations with Person B. Of King's personal attitude toward women with dark skin, Person B told me: "Martin often said he was willing to fight and die for black people, but he was damned if he could see anything pretty in a *black* woman." Person B was lighter in complexion than King. But coming out of a home where his mother appeared to be pure Negro, and coming out of an organization in which his most trusted aid, Ralph Abernathy, could not be mistaken for anything but a Negro, King's color consciousness seems to have been a direct throwback to the social values of black Atlanta.

Another person I spoke to in pursuing answers to King's life, was Mrs. Hugh Butts, née Dobbs, who grew up with M. L. She said that when the Kings moved onto Boulevard Street in Atlanta, where her own parents lived, it was a "step up for them," meaning the Kings. Ella Baker told me there had been a long-time rivalry between the Kings and the Dobbs.

Musing about King in her West Side Manhattan brownstone, Mrs. Butts saw his accumulation of degrees and roster of schools attended as "symbols" of his middle-class position. "He wanted all the right things behind his name." Says Richard

Hammer in *Commentary* (May, 1968) King was "well educated, something the Negro in the South prizes to an inordi-
nate degree."

Black people of my generation and the generation before
were taught that education is something no one can take away
from you. The emphasis in black families was on education,
and Louis Lomax states that in Georgia, "Everybody preached
against such things as adultery and stealing, but the one venial
sin was ignorance." He goes on to say that, "The education
proferred us was of a poor quality, but this was more than
overshadowed by the all but unbearable pressure that forced
us to do our studies or be literally thrashed into insensibility."

And if a young man could take graduate studies in the white
universities of the North, his status was increased manyfold.
Morehouse College has sent countless numbers of its graduates
north where an overwhelming majority of them have made
good in professional and academic circles. The A.B. soon
enough became almost nothing in terms of status; the M.A.
became the target, and, finally, the Ph.D. How grand to roll
around on the tongue the word "doctor"! How marvelous to
be addressed as "doctor"!

A man clawing out his status doesn't stop with getting an
education; there are attendant titles to earn. In the *Negro
Handbook Biographical Dictionary* (Johnson, 1966) King is
listed as an Elk and a member of Alpha Phi Alpha Fraternity.
Of the former, E. Franklin Frazier wrote: "...the Order of
Elks is a means of power and income for middle class Negroes.
...Because of the predominantly working class membership
of the Order of Elks, a middle class Negro, if he is a doctor or
college professor, will generally 'explain' his membership in
the Elks on the grounds that it is necessary for his profession,
or that he can render 'service.' "

Of the fraternities Frazier said, "It is through the Greek
letter fraternities that the so-called intellectual members of the
black bourgeoisie often gain recognition and power." Alpha

Phi Alpha is the oldest black fraternity and by that accident, the most prestigious, and a handy organization for a young man on the way up to join. I too was once a member of that fraternity, and perhaps for the very same reasons.

Status, education and otherwise, would of course have been extremely empty things without other resources. Lerone Bennett comments: "Because of their church connections and financial interests, King's grandfather and, later, his father, were members of the ruling elite of Atlanta's Negro community which was considered by some the distilled essence of what E. Franklin Frazier called the Black Puritan class." In addition, young King was heir to the fabled Ebenezer Baptist Church, which was family-owned, passing from the fiery Adam Daniel Williams to his daughter Alberta's husband, Martin King, Sr. Next in line was Martin, Jr., and last, Adam Daniel, his brother, called A. D. (A. D. drowned during a bizarre midnight swim in his pool in the summer of 1969.)

The Kings were very much a part of the Atlanta scene, had contributed its generations to its development, its standards of culture, approved generally or not, and had a vested interest in maintaining their positions in it. Lomax: "... the black South had a stout and healthy middle class society in operation. We did not think of, nor did we wish for a day when we would melt into white society."

During an interview with Bayard Rustin I said, "I'm struck by the appearance that Martin was almost always involved with the black middle class, and perhaps didn't get to the guts of the black people until Chicago. Would you agree?"

We were lunching over his desk. Downstairs, on Park Avenue South, the traffic honked and snorted its way past. Rustin chewed and thought and finally said, "Well, I think I have to agree with that, but I think that was inevitable."

That inevitability sprang naturally from his middle-class background, as determinedly achieved and as tenaciously clung to as that had been for his parents in their beginning. That he was so involved in this "society without substance," as Frazier called it, is the direct result of national white attitudes toward black people. Because those attitudes were so pronouncedly racist, it was natural that within the oppressed community there would be reflected caste systems that were also to some degree racist.

Fifteen

NOW, it is time to return again to Montgomery, where it all took hold, the *Zeitgeist*—spirit of the times, as King liked to call it—the confluence of an eager, hero-seeking press, cracker intransigence, the Supreme Court's decision of 1954 and the restlessness of American blacks. It is somehow both fitting and paradoxical that Montgomery forged the cradle of the Confederacy as well as the cradle of the contemporary civil rights movement.

All these many, many years I've wondered what would have happened there in 1954 if it had not been for the presence of Mrs. Rosa Parks, who is credited for the action that sparked the movement. She was a seamstress. This is a bland image, calling to mind the fairy tale cliché of poor but honest. I've known black seamstresses who were rich, but I don't think this was the case with Mrs. Parks. What *was* the case was her middle-class standing in the black community.

What if Mrs. Parks had not been as King wrote, "a charming" woman; what if she had not had a "radiant personality," or an "impeccable" character, or possessed a "deep-rooted" dedication? What if she had just stepped out of a bar, had not been soft-spoken but raucous; suppose her slip had been hanging and her hair a little awry, her stocking seams twisted? What if she had let the bus driver have a shot in the face with her handbag?

I think then that her attempt to gain redress against the bus company and the Southern system would have first been thwarted by the Negroes in her own community, for not being exactly the right kind of person it was willing to go to bat for. Obviously, Claudette Colvin, a student, and others before her did not completely fill the requirements for the sort of people the community leaders would support. Mrs. Parks did enjoy status in the community and, as in any community, the black leaders in Montgomery were more willing to move on behalf of a substantial citizen than an unsubstantial one.

"Fortunately," King wrote, "Mrs. Parks was ideal for the role assigned to her by history."

King's presence in Montgomery had been as carefully plotted as the presence of, say, the Kennedys in the U.S. Senate. The Dexter Avenue Baptist Church was the place where the coming big men of the black Baptist organization served; it was a step on the escalator. King himself, with barely muted pride, described that first pastorate. The church was "comparatively small, with a membership of around three hundred people, but it occupied a central place in the community. Many influential and respected citizens—professional people with substantial incomes—were among its members . . . [Dexter] was sort of a silk-stocking church catering only to a certain class. Often it was referred to as the 'big folks' church.' "

Lomax comments on Dexter: "As King well knew before he assumed the pastorate, the Dexter Avenue church did not enjoy a good reputation among Montgomery's black masses. . . . The plain implication was that nonprofessional and uneducated Negroes were not welcome at the Dexter Avenue altar. . . . It was this class discrimination in his own church, then, that first demanded Martin's attention." Lomax recalls that King's predecessor once became involved in an argument with a bus driver and then called for other black passengers to walk off the bus. "Not only did the Negroes remain in their seats, but one member of Dexter Avenue Church rebuked [the Reverend] Johns for his actions, saying, 'you should know better!' "

William Robert Miller writes more of the Dexter congregation in his biography, *Martin Luther King, Jr.:* "... the Dexter congregation included teachers from Alabama State College, as well as upper-income professionals, giving it a tone more intellectual and less emotional than the average."

Given King's upbringing, education, and his father's plans for him, King would very probably have refused to pastor a lesser church. No minister, as Lomax implies, accepts the leadership of a church without knowledge of its solvency or lack thereof, or of the composition of its congregation. King was later quoted as saying that he didn't understand the shouting and stamping, the "emotionalism" of Negro religion. It "embarrassed" him. Certainly an "intellectual" congregation appealed to him, also its financial ranking. Today's spiritual leaders do not live on faith alone. Religion is, after all, a business. The spires of the churches may stretch for the clouds, but the foundations are settled in dollars, or their pastors would like them to be.

It is not for me to say what the intellectual quality of King's congregation was at that time since I knew none of the parishioners. Intellectuals (often erroneously) tend to be associated with colleges or universities, and Alabama State College is the one King most often makes references to in *Stride.* I've never known anyone from Alabama State College, and have spoken to only one man on the faculty, and that, long after the boycott, long after King had gone on to greater fame. That professor refused to allow me to interview him because, he said, "Governor Wallace pays my salary; I have nothing to say to you."

In the cracker states the black colleges, many of which are physically similar to high schools, were established by state governments to prevent the educational development of black people. White people, of course, know this, and a growing number of black people, especially the young, are becoming aware of it. State governments sought and secured black people who were willing to abide by the rules of the system. The agreement was unwritten and unspoken; both parties simply *knew* what was being agreed to. (There were cases, however, and fortunately, when the rules were broken by the black teachers.) There could be no security for black teachers, if they did not go along with the system. Such thoroughly compromised people, in the main, have been the "intellectuals" on the faculties of the black colleges, and their major task was to provide their students with educations that could not be utilized. This is one of the reasons why, for close to a decade now, Negro students in the black colleges of crackerland have been demonstrating. They are starting to understand the system and how it operates, and they are angrily demanding a change.

James Forman's book, *Sammy Younge, Jr.* (Grove Press, 1968) details the problems black students had with their college teachers at Tuskegee, some miles north of Montgomery. The frightening part of the book is that the numbers of black teachers who collaborate with the system are not declining as rapidly as I once believed. Administrators of black colleges are on the firing line as often and as much as white college administrators—and they know it. I went to a meeting late in 1968 at which each person present had to introduce himself and present his credentials. One man did so with this phrase.

"My name is —— and I was president of —— College when I left it last night."

There was laughter, of course, but we all understood the ramifications of his statement, given the times.

There is no more telling example of King's long-time devotion to the black middle class than what happened to Montgomery after he left it. Lomax says in his *Negro Revolt:*

"Martin King left Montgomery, his work undone; the buses are integrated, but the schools are not; neither are the parks, playgrounds or other public facilities . . . one of the questions now plaguing the social scientists is why such a deep-rooted movement as the Montgomery boycott resulted in nothing more than the integration of the buses."

The answer, I think, is that the middle class in Montgomery felt it had pushed far enough; that *it* did not need open schools, parks, or playgrounds; that was a part of the unwritten contract with the system. The man in the underclass is determined to try to hold onto his dignity in the face of all the racist efforts to the contrary. The black man wishes his cup of coffee, his cheeseburger, his bus ride, his stroll through a public park, good schools for his children—to be free from the slightest hint that he possesses, or has been forced to possess, second-class citizenship. These needs are far more pressing for the black man in the street than for the middle class.

The middle-class man will eat his cheeseburger and drink his coffee in his split-level home in a middle-class neighborhood. His children and the children of his neighbors go to nearby schools, and since the neighborhood is middle class, so is the school. It goes without saying, almost, that the teachers are members in good standing of the same class. The middle-class black man will use his car for transportation, rather than suffer the daily indignity of using public transportation, and he will buy his clothes out of town so that he will not be demeaned in stores where he may not try on garments at all.

Montgomery, Alabama, had a black population of well over 45,000, or more than 35 percent of the total when King first went there. If his congregation at Dexter numbered only around 300 people, he was very possibly dealing with not the middle, but the black *upper* class of Montgomery. (Black people shy away from being considered upper class; this smacks suspiciously of behaving like Whitey.) Three hundred people do not a successful bus boycott make; nor do 5,000, which figure probably exhausted the number of middle-class blacks. Montgomery was a failure because of limited goals, uncertainty of approach, limited numbers of troops, and a failure to utilize consistently the city's entire black population.

On the other side of the coin, the white press so thoroughly indoctrinated King and his people with the idea that the capitulation of the bus company was a victory for the blacks, that they believed it; believed too that other things would inevitably fall like tin soldiers, all in a neat line.

The fact that the racist barriers did not fall down into a neat line, however, in Montgomery or anywhere else in this land, is the very reason why there is more black unity today among all classes than has ever existed before in the United States. Untold numbers of middle-class blacks have turned back to the ghetto, operating on the theory that they cannot "get loose," *i.e.*, gain a functioning place in American society, unless *all* black people gain it as well.

There is irony in the fact that Martin King was greatly, although indirectly responsible for what the white pollsters and newsmen call "the new militancy" in the black middle class. Many Negroes King's age, but generally older, believed that he was changing the racial climate for the better. The older people had children barely in their teens when the bus boycott was under way, and these youngsters moved, if not physically, at first, spiritually, with King. His nonviolent "militancy" was the *only* attack possible on the existing system; they had to go for it. Certainly there was the NAACP and the National Urban League, but these were Northern-based operations, and they chose to bang away in the courts, a time-consuming process, and one that was not guaranteed to pay off.

By 1960 the middle-class youngsters in the all-black colleges in crackerland were itching for speedier returns for practicing nonviolence than they had so far received. Perhaps having reached college age and going to institutions of higher learning sharpened their awareness. That is what college is supposed to do, and even state-supported crackerland colleges cannot escape forever what is common knowledge to everyone. Since college, at least in the United States, is the great stepping stone to middle-class life, the youngsters in the colleges automatically sought to transform things as they were into things as they wished them to be.

Although fading from memory, the Montgomery boycott nevertheless still evoked thoughts of the possibility of transferring the techniques that had made it appear to be a success to other areas of public accommodation protest. Time was fast slipping by. People who would be heard from in the early and middle sixties were emerging from their teens, people like John Lewis, Stokely Carmichael, and Rap Brown.

SNCC leaders have all come from the college-oriented middle class: Charles McDew, James Forman, John Lewis, Stokely Carmichael, and Rap Brown. Committed in the beginning to nonviolence, they were met and violently beaten. In the beginning, like their elders, they held the faith that they were dealing with a basically moral enemy. They had that faith shoved down their throats.

The "Honkie" and "Whitey" cries were born in despair, rejection, frustration, and white violence, and they did not spring first or only from the throats of Stokely or Rap. The treatment accorded SNCC was directly responsible for their formation of the Black Panthers. The leader of the most well-known group, the Oakland Panthers, is Huey P. Newton, another college-trained man, now in jail.

Older black middle-class people came to their own truths during the New York rebellion of 1964 and Watts I in 1965. There came talk that the cops were whipping black heads left and right, whether the owners of those heads were involved in the rebellions or not, or middle class or not. The talk was backed up by extensive documentation. Bread-winning middle-class blacks were being treated just like any Negro down at the pool hall. Newark and Detroit sent millions (and there are millions) of middle-class black people bounding down off the fence.

By 1967 the black middle class was apprehensively sniffing a strange, spine-tingling odor in the air. While King was still propounding nonviolence, blacks raised the question of the possibility of black genocide at the hands of whites. Some whites, too, remarked that attitudes seemed to be swinging in that direction. Quietly, and purposefully, the middle class set out on a double-pronged venture. Return to the ghetto; unite with the man in the street. Supply him with help, education, encouragement—anything he needed to be a completely functioning man. And: Obtain arms. Although the white middle class is far, far ahead of the blacks in this respect, if Armageddon comes, there are going to be a number of very, very surprised white people. I hope black people have been trained well enough not to be surprised by whites, for there are many surprises lying in wait there, too.

Joanne Grant, who reported on every aspect of the movement for many years, explained why King and black leaders generally, "except the kids," had concentrated on the middle class. "They do not trust or respect ordinary people. They're afraid of them, and they think they're stupid."

So, in view of King's thoroughly middle-class background, his penchant for moving with and doing things for the middle class is not to be condemned; it is to be understood in the light of American society and subsociety. Perhaps King's friend, Louis Lomax, best summed up King's inbred inability to relate to the black underclass in his *To Kill a Black Man*.

"What caused Watts to explode?" King had asked on his tour there shortly after Watts I.

After Lomax and other supplied him with the answers, Lomax "realized then that Martin did not fully understand in his guts the madness induced by ghetto life."

The following year, 1966, when King had moved into the westside ghetto in Chicago, Lomax noted, "After a month there Martin noticed a chilling change in his children; they became sullen and hostile; they would not obey. His son became outright defiant. With no place to play, being constantly surrounded by hopelessness and despair, the King child absorbed the syndrome of the ghetto. It was only a matter of time before they too would begin throwing bricks and fashioning Molotov cocktails. The children were shipped back home to the fresh air of black middle class America."

Sixteen

We live in a success-oriented society, and we are all aware of it, from the blondest, blue-eyed white boy, to the blackest, kinky-haired Negro boy. But we also live in a society where that success must be gained at the expense of others. Webster defines success as being the prosperous termination of any enterprise; a person, or thing, which achieves favor or gain. This definition hints at the accumulation of wealth, which is the preoccupation of a capitalistic society. In fact, white people take success to mean exactly that.

On the other hand, black people all too often have equated success with widespread publicity. Sometimes the very sharp differences are blurred by the public at large. Success as a public man in America depends in great part in being sought out by other public men. Thus, King's success was partially a result of the attention paid him by Presidents and others who actually were in a position to wield power in his behalf. But success in this nation is a very dangerous thing. I define popular success as being recognized by large numbers of people as prime movers in and of society. Popular success is a two-way street. The accolades coming from the people seem to confer a license to act on their behalf. The person receiving them does not have to accept that license. But if he does, then he has become a full partner to his own creation—the creation of the winner, the successful public man.

The powers that abide in the United States are past masters at castrating the enemies of the establishment under the guise of honoring them (the enemies are all, and almost without exception, operating in the area of sociopolitical improvement), or, at least, of airing their side of the story on television, in magazine articles, or making public appearances available to them.

Traveling through black Africa, Egypt, the Sudan, and parts of Israel, I noticed that many people ran from the aimed camera; others flew into fury, and after a while I let my camera hang idly around my neck. If I wanted a picture badly enough, I'd ask permission to take it, even at the risk of losing the spontaneity that might have been captured in a candid. I tend to agree, in a secret way, with those people, that exposure *does* allow something of the spirit to seep out—to pass into the possession of the photographer—and I am now talking about all kinds of exposure.

We have all seen over the years the more vocal and furious black leaders, local and national, spread across the television screen on the seven and eleven o'clock news, have read countless articles and news stories about Martin King, Malcolm X, Stokely Carmichael, Rap Brown, and Le Roi Jones. While exposure to the white masses proved them to be just as human as the next man, that same exposure whipped up—just as it was designed to—a kind of phony fear.

Most people did not, and would not today, consider Martin King in the same category as the men I mentioned above, as an enemy of the establishment. The answer to that is a question: *Then why is he dead?*

Then why is he dead, in what writer Paul Good says is a "tragedy that suggests at least a fateful accident of timing?"

There is another kind of success. The adulation does not come from the masses, but from peer groups. The most powerful men in the United States, and I do not necessarily include the President (especially not Richard M. Nixon), although the office is generally acknowledged to be synonymous with power, are not public men. And they are the prime movers. They do not make the covers of the mass magazines, and they don't ever intend to make them. You don't find them sitting at tables, the targets of television cameras, and you don't read many articles about them, if any at all. True power has a vested interest in secrecy.

The popular success that appears to grant unlimited power is a pitfall whose bottom is covered with upright, sharpened stakes; it becomes a gorgeous woman who is filled to bursting with gonococci. The public man is expendable. He is in the first instance conceived to be destroyed or shunted aside when another is deemed to be more suitable.

But public attention is heady, very heady stuff, and few people can resist it when it comes. We want to be known. None of us wishes to come into this world and pass from it without leaving a very distinctive trail behind. Having children will not do; that is the commonplace route to the most modest kind of immortality. We must be known as someone far above the ordinary cut of men.

Martin King was twenty-six years old when world attention came to him. But then, he expected some adulation. An associate of the King family says:

"Martin Luther King, Sr., was a social-climber. Pushy. Aggressive. As far as the family was concerned. He wanted them to be big stuff. He wanted to prove himself about the whole thing. They suffer from that psychology in Atlanta—rich [black] people—of placing a good deal of emphasis on money and social position, on public esteem and doing the right thing and being in the right places and going to the right schools, knowing the right people.

"The mother, too. Very, very aggressive. I considered him [M. L. King, Sr.] to be a bit of a fool in that sense. Somehow or other they managed to pick on Martin, Jr., as the one to push. Maybe he was very bright when he was a little kid, and they always seemed to push him from then, as I understand it, to be something, to the neglect of A. D. [Albert Daniel, King's brother]."

Is there a man who goes into the ministry who does not wish to "be something"? But to walk to the podiums confronting vast halls, to slouch casually before batteries of microphones and television cameras, to be seen and heard—the spirit ranging far and wide—by immeasurably large audiences is a situation the great majority of people, black and white, are not trained up to. Oratory and Martin King were mentioned in one breath; recall the face in photographs and hear once again in memory, the measured, Georgian cadence, the sinking and rising soft black voice, the imagery often sharp, but generally merely adequate. And you do become aware of a sense of seeming power over a responsive audience that, between your pauses for breath, overwhelms you with its empathy, its attention to your presence, voice, words. I've experienced the sense; there is nothing quite like it. You feel when they break in upon you with applause, or when they allow you palpably to touch their attentiveness, that you can take the world, as is, with their total consent, and do just as you wish. It is a mystical experience, and a man can easily be deluded into thinking that what the audience is giving back is power that will run endlessly on into time.

Martin King grew up addressing large black audiences, mostly connected with his church or, later, college. Lomax recalls that his father, as President of the Georgia Baptist Training Union Convention, "gave Martin, then in his early teens, his first statewide platform on 'Christian Youth' night." Young King was already beckoning for a public before it was to become his. Some set of common circumstances must go into the makeup of the minister, actor, and politician. We have seen that the parts are interchangeable. Each knows from the moment he first charts his public course that if successful, he will almost always be in the public eye. It is perhaps this more than anything else that initially attracted him to his calling, though he cannot admit this or will not.

The politician states modestly that he wishes to serve the people. The minister wishes to serve God through helping the people. The actor wishes to bring pleasure to the people. They each state concern for the people. Such concern over the generations past would have made us a far better people than we are now. One must admire such unselfishness, but deplore the truth of the situation, for it is paradoxically the height of selfishness.

Some men, whether or not they've made their concern for others public, accept adulation gracefully, if they are public men. Others, having accepted it, come to a time when they are eager to reject it in secret ways; they plead to be rediscovered as ordinary men. What they truly wish, of course, is to have the tune played without having to pay the piper. They wish the power, or what seems to be power, without the responsibilities that go with even the illusion. Illusions can sometimes be made real. Martin King refused that opportunity. It is common knowledge that he was not the field general he could have been.

But Ella Baker points out a profound and mortal weakness of King's organization: "It was composed of ministers, none of whom had had enough organizational experience, other than the church which, basically, is not an experience in building an organization. Because a minister comes in and all he does is maybe change the head of the Sunday school, or change the head of the Pastor's Aid Society, or he might add two more names to some other part of the board. But the basic pattern has not changed."

King was not an organizer; this is why Bayard Rustin remained enduringly in the picture, in the wings; and this is why Ella Baker remained in the wings, too.

Joanne Grant, a classmate of mine at Syracuse University, sat in her apartment talking to me about King, and about the movement and all her years of covering it for the *National Guardian*. Joanne (Mrs. Victor Rabinowitz) was pregnant, and it was a hot spring morning, muggy as only New York can be. If Joanne were not black (she is really beige in complexion) she could have been a top newswoman, but we didn't talk about that, being contemporaries, more or less, and knowing what both of us had gone through; we were talking instead about King, and now we were on King's lack of organizational ability:

"It was very important to him that he should make the decisions, and yet he really couldn't. He wasn't able to think things through and make up his own mind. Yet he held the organization under his thumb, partially by hand-picked advisers. If somebody was too strong, he wouldn't want him around. Even those who were bright and strong became real followers."

Time magazine for January 3, 1964, in which King was named Man of the Year, noted that "King has neither the quiet brilliance nor the sharp administrative capabilities of the N.A.A.C.P.'s Roy Wilkins ... none of the sophistication of the Urban League's Whitney Young, Jr.... he has neither the inventiveness of CORE's James Farmer nor the raw militancy of SNICK's John Lewis nor the bristling wit of Author James Baldwin...."

Had King been able to organize, expand, and control more effectively the destiny of SCLC, he could have turned the illusion of power and success into significant reality, although many black people insist that it could never become more than what it was—a group of preachers with differing goals.

Modern communications make it a foregone conclusion that the man who is a popular success here at home, will be recognized as such abroad. There King's popularity increased by leaps and bounds, particularly after the March on Washington. Europeans have generally been kind to American blacks who were public victims of racism or who fought it. They offered asylum to many, Richard Wright being the most illustrious black refugee. (But the French grew weary of him, and the British would not give him a permanent visa to live in London.)

Distance from the problem has made the Europeans, at

least superficially, benevolent. Rare, however, is the west European nation that has not been profitably involved in the exploitation of nonwhites. Like so many other Negroes, once on the far shores of the Atlantic, King minimized or neglected to remind Europeans that their guilt was as great as America's. The attention lavished on King in Europe tended to reinforce the illusion of his power. And why not? Why shouldn't Europeans have catered to him? At that time King may have held in his hands the fate of not only the United States, but of western Europe as well.

Chester Himes, who has lived in Europe for nearly twenty years, points out that, should the United States become embroiled in nationwide racial rebellions over an extended period, the European economy, which is closely aligned with ours, would suffer extensively. "America cannot afford to fall out, not only on account of the economic balance of the world which is so sensitive; they cannot afford any enmity with all the nations with whom they collaborate. . . . I think if the white man had to take the choice between giving the black man his rights or destroying the entire economic system through black rebellions because he won't allow the Negro to share in that system, he'd give the black man his equality."

As American ballyhoo tended to inflate King's image as a power to be reckoned with, so European interest for all its either ignorant or dishonest reasons, bolstered his prestige at home. First Kennedy and then Johnson learned from Eisenhower's refusal to invite King to tea. But King's critics contend that he traded tea with the Presidents for the guts of the movement; then he, as well as other leaders, sought only personal prestige when they sat in the White House, and that that prestige did not rub off in palpable gains for black Americans.

Joanne Grant remembers when a group of black leaders descended on the White House during the Kennedy regime, to be addressed by the President:

"He said, 'You've got to have patience. I'm not going to

promise you anything. I'll do the best I can; you have to understand the problem.' And then Kennedy took us on a tour of the White House and showed us Lincoln's bedroom. LINCOLN'S BEDROOM! It was so insulting! But those big guns got right on that train and talked all the way to Philadelphia about their conference at the White House."

And Rap Brown in his book, *Die Nigger Die!* (The Dial Press, 1969) comments on what happens when the "leaders" acting for their people, go to a White House meeting:

> It was the time of the Selma March when people were beaten up on Pettus Bridge. We had a delegation to go see Johnson. . . . we went to see Johnson in this big conference room that had this conference table about two miles long. About 20 members comprised the delegation, white and Negro. When we went in, everybody sat down and then Johnson came in. From the jump, the leader of the delegation who is now one of the boys in charge of Washington, D.C., went into his act. Soon as "the man" got there, he started grinning and laughing. He had this statement written out and he passed it across the table to Johnson. Johnson was arrogant as hell and mad 'cause we were there. . . . Well, he looked at the statement and didn't even read it. He just threw it back across the table. Threw it back!
>
> After that, each member of the delegation introduced himself and said a few words. The dude from the NAACP got up and said, "Mr. President, it really is a pleasure to be here. This will be something that I'll be proud to tell my children and grandchildren about." Then came another fool who said the same thing.
>
> . . . Well, it was my time and I'm really pissed off by this time. . . . So I told him . . . "We are interested in the lives of our people. Which side is the federal government on?" I looked around and the bootlickers were getting scared. . . . When we came out, all them jive Toms and all them old white folks come running round telling me what a good job I had done and that it was good that I had done that.

James Forman, now head of the National Black Economic Development Conference, Air Force veteran, graduate of

Roosevelt College and a student at Boston University, as well as SNCC executive secretary from 1961 to 1966, perceived that White House meetings were futile and that the participants who were black were primarily seeking personal stature. When the White House called his office to notify him of meetings there with other black leaders, he snapped to his secretary: "I'm out of town."

"Power," Frederick Douglass often said, "concedes nothing without demand."

Since the death of Martin King, thousands of "demands" have been issued by black militants and revolutionaries. The establishment has ignored many of these and paid token attention to others. The establishment knows that there are only two bases from which power can spring. The first is money, which black people do not have in anywhere near adequate sums to buy politicians, buy media, buy influence. The second is a cohesive, national organization of people who by their numbers, attitudes, and threatening posture evolve into a force for power.

Everyone near King for the years he marched through American history, from Bayard Rustin, to Ella Baker, to James Lawson, to a multitude of SNCC people, told him that his drive to gain open public accommodations was going to be in vain; that his goals were too intangible. They told him that his target should be political power and that could only come through black unification. But perhaps even the time for that is past.

The years 1968 and 1969 beheld the general rise of conservative city administrations in the United States. These were made possible and will continue to be possible because of "metropolitanism," which means that city governments expand into the suburbs to which whites have fled, performing services and raking in taxes, but, most important, bringing great numbers of whites back to the voting booths to offset the effect of the blacks in the ghettos. In other words, "metropolitanism" is just one more white exercise in rendering the ghettos powerless. The current times also brought in Richard Nixon, a two-time loser, on a fear-provoked conservative binge. Obviously running roughshod over the supporters of school desegregation, his administration even sparked a brief revolt among the younger attorneys in the Justice Department. Yet by early fall, 1969, under the eyes and ears of a very lazy or perhaps uncaring national press, black children, who the year before had attended the South's few desegregated schools, were having those same doors slammed in their faces.

Mr. Nixon had set the tone and the crackers have run to sing the chorus.

This is to say, of course, that black people have no power, and white people are not going to give or share it with them. The evidence litters our history like skeletons in a desert. Indeed, King may have missed seeing the beginning of the end of the Second Reconstruction, which, like the first, promised equal stature to black citizens on paper, but failed completely to deliver.

But Martin King was alive during the Adam Clayton Powell episode, which smacked of the post-Reconstruction era when black Congressmen were refused their seats. Although the Supreme Court ruled that Congress had no right to deprive him of his seat, many Congressmen echoed the thought of the man who said, "Okay, they've ruled. Now let them enforce it."

Martin King did not comprehend the capriciousness of white power. Although at times he showed himself to be an eager student of American history, black and white, at other times he exhibited a deplorable lack of awareness of its significance in regard to black people.

"Martin," Person B told me, "was nothing but a Southern country boy, naïve as hell about almost everything."

King, believing he had power, attacked the white power structure. He did not understand that it had armed him with feather dusters. While he may have believed that the Nobel

Prize brought him even more power, he returned home to be vilified, spat on, and struck with rocks. He was a black man and therefore always was and always would be naked of power, for he was slow—indeed unable—to perceive the manipulation of white power, and in the end white power killed him.

Seventeen

AND so, Montgomery, and for King, public recognition. No matter that he pastored a church that, along with its parishioners, was unpopular with the local black masses. No matter that no one is especially eager to talk about the meeting at which King was elected president of the Montgomery Improvement Association. Nor did it matter, as James Meredith said, that the philosophy of nonviolence was not then thought out. "All the thinking came after."

True. "Noncooperation" became nonviolence, became even later the doctrine of Satyagraha, which attempted to reveal the suffering, made deliberate, of man, in order that society would be forced to respect and secure the rights of those made to suffer. Satyagraha holds that the state does not possess unlimited authority, even if created by the majority of people. The state tends inevitably to violate the rights of the individual.

Raghavan N. Iyer, writing in the Center for the Study of Democratic Institutions magazine issue on Civil Disobedience, sums up Satyagraha:

"In essence [it] emphasizes that social and political conflicts can be handled best in an atmosphere in which the contestants respect the moral worth of each other, distinguish between measures and persons, conduct their battles in a spirit of self-criticism, and abstain from the cruder forms of coercion."

It did not matter that it took King so long to get this together, as long as he finally did. The press had made its decision, and King had agreed to agree with it. Lomax notes that even before the conclusion of the boycott King had decided that he could never return to the pastorate, "the pastorate alone."

It was at that moment of decision, or of contract signing—for, that decision was, for King, tantamount to signing the contract to become a public man—that he should have reread his own words that he'd written in his doctoral thesis only two years before: "The more fully any object prehends the rest of being, the more it is subject to the destructive works of evil. The higher we rise in the levels of prehension, the greater place there is for the destructive works of evil."

Montgomery was important to black people, even if its success was illusory. It was most important to Martin King for extremely personal reasons, and again his boyhood friend, Lomax, attempts to explain why:

"I am not suggesting open conflict between Martin and his father, but I am calling attention to the fact that such men as Martin Luther King, Sr. are so strong and hard driving that they traditionally are all but impossible to live with. Such men tend to confuse their own desires with God's will and the sons who bear their names spend the first quarter of their lives trying to establish their own manhood in a manner that will not alienate their fathers."

Thus, a man in his own right, and licensed by the American press, King went to Albany, Georgia, in 1962 with Wyatt Tee Walker who would organize what SNCC and the NAACP kids had already organized; King would lend his new prestige to the drive to desegregate the bus terminal, although his presence was deeply resented. Albany was the home of Albany State College for blacks, and was near an Army base. It was vulnerable in that its sins, like those of most towns, were worn on its sleeve.

Of course, any city that maintains segregation of its public accommodations, maintains segregation in other areas. Once the drive was mounted in Albany, all segregated institutions there came under fire. The cry went out for the hiring of black policemen, equal job opportunities, a standing black-white committee to deal with racial problems—in short, a complete change in the Southern way of life in Albany.

Whether he had been invited or not—and this was always a bone of contention that was worried whenever King appeared and either joined or commenced a campaign—he went to Albany and was arrested four times. Two thousand demonstrators went to jail with him. During his last arrest King vowed to stay in jail until the demands of the blacks were met, hotting up the already tense situation.

"But that was what he was for," a veteran of the campaign told me. "He was the cat who put the whole operation on his own back."

King's statement about staying in jail crackled out and temporarily stilled the differences between SNCC, the NAACP, and SCLC; black people drew together, restless and fearing King's fate in that Georgia countryside jail. "Creative tension," the phrase King was to later utilize, was everywhere evident. Blacks moved sullenly through Albany's streets and one report had the black GI's at the nearby base ready with hidden arms. White Albany officials feared that backcountry elements might one night decide to storm the jail where King was and lynch him, as they had done with other blacks of far lesser stature. Louis Lomax was there and recorded: "Then Martin Luther King changed his mind. He had promised that he would stay in jail until a change came; he invited others to come and spend Christmas in jail with him. Had he stuck to this, as Ghandi would have done, Albany would have been desegregated. But Martin came out on bond."

"Sellout!"

"Uncle Tom Nigger!"

"Jive Cat!"

"Martin Loser!"

Those were the charges. The image was tarnished on its

second major outing. Why, *why* did King himself wind down the creative tension that could have provided an altogether different ending to the Albany story?

Lomax, who covered the Albany campaign and suggested in *The Negro Revolt* (Harper & Row, 1962) that he had information that could shed light on King's actions, did just that in *To Kill a Black Man.* Continuing the Albany story, he says that one of the local black leaders jailed with King became mentally ill while in jail, and King accepted bond in order to take the man out with him so he could receive treatment. According to Lomax, "Martin and others of those jailed conferred and agreed that it would be disastrous for the movement if the white jailer discovered and informed the world that one of the key local black leaders was mentally ill." The man refused to free himself on bond as long as King remained in jail.

Whites tend to believe Albany was a disaster for King. Most blacks agree, but not for the same reason. King's failure in the first place, black people contend, was not that he came out of jail at a crucial moment, but that he had not dealt in political realities at all. Desegregation, they said, could come and remain as a lasting influence only through political power—not through moral persuasion.

On the other hand, there were small signs that radical elements of the Protestant and Catholic churches and the synagogues as well had become convinced of the validity of nonviolent resistance, and many appeared on the Albany scene, some too briefly, and all too few anyway, to significantly influence their respective churches.

A newsmagazine cable in fact noted:

"A promised visitation of one hundred white and Negro ministers from other states to protest the jailing of King and Albany's stubborn stand, did not materialize as of late last week. A handful of ministers showed up, visited King in his cell in the city jail, attended the mass rallies, but did not demonstrate themselves."

Albany is most important because it was here that King, grossly underestimating J. Edgar Hoover and his Bureau, complained about its agents, calling directly down on his head (which he may have thought invulnerable by now) the wrath of an offended govermental agency. Demonstrators had charged the Albany police with brutality and notified the FBI, only to become immediately disenchanted with the Bureau's response. King then advised his people not to lodge any more complaints of brutality with the FBI. He said, "One of the greatest problems we face with the FBI in the South is that the agents are white Southerners who have been influenced by the mores of the community. To maintain their status, they have to be friendly with local police and people who are permitting segregation. . . . If an FBI man agrees with segregation, he can't honestly and objectively investigate."

Then, his remarks recorded for the press, Martin King moved on to Birmingham.

One of the main affiliates of SCLC in Birmingham was the Reverend Fred Shuttlesworth's Alabama Christian Movement for Human Rights. Shuttlesworth was perhaps the best of the lot of the ministers in SCLC. Black journalists held him in high regard. Joanne Grant describes him: "Shuttlesworth was more honest, more intelligent, more courageous, a better organizer, a better grass-roots leader than King was. He had faults, of course, the main one being that he was unable to share responsibility. Shuttlesworth tended to equate the movement with himself."

King, too, would praise Shuttlesworth, but *after* the campaign. As at Albany, the fact that King and SCLC were in Birmingham preparing to mount massive demonstrations was enough to set Washington and the Kennedy brothers on edge. King had characterized the city as the toughest in the nation in terms of segregation. And Roy Wilkins had let it be known that the Negroes of Birmingham were among the roughest in America. This was patently a contradiction, for had they been as rough as Wilkins said, King would not have been needed. April 12, Good Friday, 1963. Martin King and his perennial companion, Ralph Abernathy, were locked up in Birmingham jail and no word of their condition had been received by Wyatt Tee Walker, Coretta King, or Shuttlesworth. Mrs. King set out to track down President Kennedy. The following evening Kennedy called Mrs. King.

There was in that sequence of events the appearance of a game. King is jailed. No word is received from him. Mrs. King, with a direct pipeline to the President or his aides, calls for help. The minions of the administration react. The FBI checks the Birmingham jail and reports that King is in fine shape, suffering nothing more than the petty sadistic treatment every black man suffers behind bars. But even that treatment ceases when the FBI comes in, just checking, and King marvels that his treatment at the hands of the guards has quickly and inexplicably improved.

With King in jail and demonstrators piling up in the main streets by the thousands, creative tension is stretched to the limit, mostly by the use of police dogs employed by the police. Bobby Kennedy takes charge in Washington, soliciting the aid of such administration people as Douglas Dillon of Treasury, Eugene Rostow of Yale Law School, Secretary McNamara and Burke Marshall of Justice.

Eight days after their arrest, King and Abernathy accept their freedom on $300 cash bond "in order to consult with the movement's strategy committee," says Miller. "I had decided to put into operation a new phase of our campaign, which I felt would speed victory," said King.

Mayhem continues in the streets. King's brother, A. D., has his home bombed; the motel where King himself was staying is bombed, but he was in Atlanta at the time, but the demonstrations and marches continue, Dick Gregory, Andrew Young, and A. D. King taking up the slack whenever King and Shuttlesworth were absent from the streets.

And finally, it all seemed to be over. The movement had

pressed for four moderate points: the desegregation of lunch counters, etc.; the upgrading and hiring of blacks on a non-discriminatory basis; the dropping of all charges against demonstrators who had been jailed, and the creation of a biracial committee to set forth a timetable for desegregation throughout Birmingham.

The movement's demands were met—with strings attached: "within ninety days," "within sixty days," etc. Nowhere is there mentioned the application of the law, and so the demands that were made and agreed to remained in a vacuum, dependent upon the moral sense of the Birmingham community—a community that reacted with the bombings, not only of the King brothers, but of the twenty-four black girls, four of whom died in their Sunday school classroom.

In such an atmosphere, victory was pyrrhic. John Kennedy in Washington could say at a news conference that everything was working out, and Martin King could claim a victory, but novelist John O. Killens, himself a father, could say at the funeral of the girls that nonviolence was dead. A lot of black people agreed with him, but then, a lot of black people saw the demands that had been agreed to as sham, unenforceable and shuck of the first magnitude, for as one resident said, "Not only was there nothing you could lay your hand to, it was plain that as soon as Birmingham got off television and the front pages, it would be business as usual. Martin Luther King, being an intelligent man and a Georgia boy, should've been the first one to know that."

Toward the end of the Birmingham campaign I said in the *New Leader* (May 27, 1963): "The last players in this continuing game of charades very likely will be the people Dr. King does not have in his fold. The rioting was kicked off by Negroes terribly unwilling, as King suggested, to let their blood flow instead of their white brothers'. These are the people the South most fears. Sullen, deprived, outside the community of religion and economic influences, they are prepared to meet violence with violence; they are the people fabled in Southern story as 'bad niggers.'... Raised on a heritage of violence without the soothing ministrations of the church, they are willing to dispense violence themselves."

King refused to admit that black violence could get past his own philosophy. When Killens declared that nonviolence was dead, King denied that it was.

People wanted to be with King and he knew it. No one wants to have his life constantly on the line; our minds are not prepared for it in what is known as a peaceful society. Yet they also knew that Killens was right, had to be right, because each and every black man knew that nonviolence was like a cinder in the violent eye of white America. Did King himself have some brooding doubts about his philosophy after the Freedom Rides, after Albany and now, after Birmingham?

Meredith: "I've always believed that he didn't really believe in it; it was just a tactic. In fact, he told me so. He was not sure it was the answer."

King had told a *Look* senior editor, Ernest Dunbar, in an interview February 12, 1963, that he believed in a "militant, nonviolent approach, in which the individual stands up against an unjust system, using sit-ins, legal action, boycotts, votes and everything else—except violence or hate."

The key word in King's quote, is of course, "militant." What follows is totally contradictory, for "militant" means combative, aggressive, engaged in warfare or strife. When the press cites a black as being militant, it is saying that he is aggressive, seeks white blood. Unfortunately, we all adopt the vocabulary of the media without examining the meaning of the words. But I have no doubt that King meant exactly what he said and was aware of the word's basic meaning.

Birmingham was the turning point. No longer would nonviolence be the supreme, unquestioned philosophy or policy for black people seeking their share of America; and in the North, Malcolm X was making sure of that, downgrading King's every campaign.

More important perhaps was the observation that prayers or prayer preceded every act of every campaign. The prayers signaled to observers that the demonstrators had a great deal less faith in their marches than they should have had. The pattern, of course, was established by Martin King.

For a fleeting moment in Birmingham it appeared that the black middle-class businessmen would reject King's almost nonrole and become a positive economic force in the movement. I express this view in the same *New Leader* article:

"The Negro business community of the South may now be inclined to get off the fence. It has been about as moderate about desegregation as white business groups. . . . Negro businesses within the segregated community, insurance particularly, have created black millionaires. . . . If [A. G.] Gaston's cooperation and help and money has come to the aid of the desegregation efforts, a new phase in Negro staying power may be at hand, for millions of dollars are available."

That was 1963. I was mistaken, failing to realize that black businessmen, like businessmen anywhere, tend to be, if not conservative, cautious. No businessman yet has discovered how to make a profit out of civil rights demonstrations.

But 1963 was Martin King's year, nonetheless—in more ways than one. With Albany and then Birmingham, he had genuinely irritated Washington, and its people were going to respond.

Eighteen

HOW were they going to respond and for what reason?

The reason they were going to respond was that while many believed that King had become "more a symbol than a power in the civil rights movement," as August Meier says, there was always the chance—growing with every campaign—that King could wind up with a genuine power to couple with his prestige.

In Howard Sackler's play, *The Great White Hope*, the FBI agent, Dixon, sets forth succinctly why black images must be destroyed. He speaks of Jack Jefferson (or the first black world's heavyweight boxing champion, Jack Johnson):

When a man beats us out like this, we—the law, that is—
suffer in prestige, and that's pretty serious.
How people regard the law is part of its effectiveness,
it can't afford to look foolish, and this applies
especially now to our Negro population.
I don't mean just the ones who always flout the law,
and seeing their hero doing it in style
act up more than usual—those are police concerns, not ours.
But though you may not be aware of it yet, a very large, very black
migration is in progress.
They're coming from the fields down there and filling up
the slums,
trouble's starting in Europe, and our mills and factories
have work for them now. And I'm talking of hundreds

of thousands, maybe millions soon—
millions of ignorant Negroes, rapidly massing together,
their leanings, their mood, their outlook, suddenly
no longer regulated by the little places they come from—
situations have arisen already.
We cannot allow the image of this man
to go on impressing and exciting these people.*

It was not until 1968, after King's death, that we learned
how those people in Washington responded; they had their
reason. Drew Pearson and Jack Anderson wrote in that 1968
column of theirs that on July 16, 1963, the Birmingham campaign over but a matter of weeks, Attorney General Robert F.
Kennedy "ordered a wiretap put on the phone." That phone
belonged to Martin King. According to Pearson and Anderson, the tap was not placed, however, until October, 1963.
I make the ordinary assumption that from that time until his
death, King was under government surveillance not so that it
might offer him protection, but for purposes running counter
to the movement's.

What excuse was given to permit the authorization of wire-
tapping King's office?

In a telephone conversation I had with Jack Newfield,
author of *Robert Kennedy, A Memoir* (E. P. Dutton, 1969),
he said that he'd questioned Kennedy about the Pearson-
Anderson report that he had signed an order to place the tap
on King's phone. Off the record Kennedy told Newfield that
he had signed the order at Hoover's insistence because of
the presence on the SCLC staff of Jack O'Dell, an editor of
Freedomways magazine, who reportedly had Communist
connections.

But, according to Lionel Lokos' *House Divided* (Arlington

* In Robert Lipsyte's Saturday column, "Sports of the Times," in the New
York *Times,* he wrote on November 29, 1969, about Muhammad Ali: "Then
came Cassius, confident, skilled, proud of his blackness, and the 'power structure' saw it would have trouble if black men were allowed to identify with
him."

Lipsyte was writing about a film interview with the late Malcolm X.

House, 1968), O'Dell left SCLC on friendly terms and by mutual agreement on *June 26, 1963.* This was *after* Kennedy himself had spoken to King, according to Newfield, and warned him to get rid of O'Dell. King then spoke to O'Dell, and a mutual and warm decision was made for the latter to leave the organization. After three months, Kennedy rescinded the order. But, and still according to Newfield, J. Edgar Hoover ordered a *bug* placed in the SCLC offices. By the time Robert Kennedy discovered it, his brother had been murdered in Dallas, and Hoover, as he'd done before Robert Kennedy became Attorney General, reported directly to the President, now Lyndon B. Johnson.

There are several holes in Kennedy's "off the record" statement to Newfield. The first being that if O'Dell had already left SCLC, why was the tap necessary since O'Dell's presence had been the "reason" for placing it in the first place?

Second, did Hoover really defy Kennedy and place the bug in the office? If this is so, then the Attorney General, like others before him, lacked the power to prevent Hoover from doing anything he wished to do. On the other hand, Newfield says that Kennedy was the first Attorney General to make Hoover report directly to him.

Third, if Kennedy was kind enough to warn King to rid himself of O'Dell, why didn't he warn King of the bug in his offices as soon as he learned of it?

The machinery had been set in motion to compromise or break the man the press and the attendant powers had created.

"I knew Martin Luther King as a man."
"Yes," I said, "but what does that mean?" She was extremely fair and had freckles. Her answer was a giggle.

Person D

July, 1963. Fresh from Birmingham, feted nationwide and invited to head demonstrations all over the country, King went to Danville, Virginia, to lend his support to the civil rights drives there. It was coming too thick and too fast: He went to Atlanta to keep SCLC tightened up and in the center of things, then to various other cities, and at the same time he was commuting between Danville and New York, where he was helping to plan the March on Washington.

William Robert Miller lists what went on during that single year:

"Nine hundred and thirty demonstrations occurred in at least 115 Southern cities, in which King's arrest in Birmingham was one of 20,083 that occurred throughout 11 Southern states. Thirty-five bombings were known to have occurred in 1963. The annual balance sheet of the Southern Regional Council also noted "some progress toward integration" in 186 localities, and continuing negotiations in 102 of them by biracial committees, which could be expected to result in further strides toward freedom."

It was natural that after such a widespread drive toward civil rights a culminating demonstration should be held.

It was a warm pleasant August day, and driving through Washington, I had the impression that, save for the black sections of town, it was empty. I stopped at the press tent near the Lincoln Memorial; the marchers had not yet set out from the Washington Monument. Word was going around there that march leaders considered the speech John Lewis planned to give as too belligerent. The Most Reverend Patrick J. O'Boyle, Archbishop of the Roman Catholic Archdiocese of Washington, had been the person most opposed to Lewis' speech, and he threatened not deliver the invocation if the "inflammatory" sections of it were not deleted. One disputed passage read: "We will not wait for the President, the Justice Department nor the Congress, but we will take matters into our own hands and create a source of power, outside any national structure, that could and would assure us a victory. . . ."

(In 1963 words like those horrified white allies; in 1969,

they are so passé that no one bothers to speak them anymore; what Lewis threatened is already in motion.)

Other leaders of the march, urgently seeking a show of unanimity, apparently sided with O'Boyle, for the section was deleted. John Lewis was twenty-five then, the youngest of the ten leaders present. He'd been arrested twice as many times as King—even at that point. Since his name *wasn't* King, when he went to jail, telephone lines didn't burn up between where he was and Washington. He's been in on the sit-ins, the Freedom Rides, and he was SNCC's third chairman. In 1965, in many of the photographs taken on the Selma march, Lewis could be seen in the foreground with a knapsack on his back at Pettus Bridge when blacks first attempted to cross it and were cossacked down. Pictures taken only minutes later show him on the ground holding his head, the cracker cops riding past on their horses.

After Washington, the youngsters in particular, gave King low marks for not supporting Lewis' right to free speech; others say he supported him, but it is clear that if he had, Lewis would have delivered his talk exactly as he'd written it. Lewis' speech would have been a direct challenge to the genteel tone of the demonstration. He wanted to say that he was tired of waiting, would wait no longer. King set his own talk in the never-never realm of "I have a dream." King achieved his goal of bringing his nonviolent philosophy before the largest possible audience, but what John Lewis did *not* say that day was at the guts of the issue. John Lewis loomed larger than his fellow-leaders. He could have walked off the program, but he chose to stay on, presenting that neat, harmonious picture so desperately wished for by the leaders of the march. Even under censorship, he gave the most militant speech of the day.

At about the time Martin King and other leaders were gathering in the White House, congratulating themselves on the success of the march, a wealthy tobacco farmer, William

Zantzinger of Maryland, received his sentence for caning a black barmaid to death. Few of the marchers had taken the time to discover that, for the beating of Mrs. Hattie Carroll, Zantzinger was given a six-month sentence and fined $625. His confinement was to be delayed until September 15 to allow him to finish gathering his tobacco crop.

I stood among a group of marchers who watched the leaders prepare to make their triumphal journey to the White House. An old lady, dressed in her Sunday best, remarked, "Well, I guess this is one time Dr. King decided to stick around until the end of the dance."

"Maybe," someone else said, "that's because there was no head beating and tearing up the streets."

The record revealed that during every demonstration in which King participated, at the key moment when he was most acutely needed to lead a mass confrontation, he was absent.

Miller notes this: "When local movements built themselves around King, they let themselves in for a powerful vacuum in his absence." Miller goes on to defend King: "He did not realize this, but he could have done little about it in any case."

Obviously, the old woman in Washington felt otherwise, and she wasn't the only one who did.

"Martin wasn't careful. He just didn't care. Reckless. He'd wear a pair of sunglasses and think no one could recognize him. One night we were in this restaurant in Riverdale, and a man came up and said how pleased he was that he could meet Reverend King in person. Martin sat right there and held a little conversation with him. He introduced me as his cousin.

Person B

October was the month when, according to Pearson and Anderson, the tap on King's telephone went into effect. Their reports of taps and bugs would be corroborated in 1969 when

FBI agents would testify in Houston, Texas, that they had indeed tapped the telephones—and for periods of several years —not only of Martin King, but of Elijah Muhammad, head of the Black Muslims, and Muhammad Ali, "former" heavyweight boxing champion.

Back in November, 1962, in Albany, Georgia, King had sharply criticized Hoover's agency. The director of the FBI is reputed to have an ominously long memory, and he probably —if Newfield's statement is correct—went along delightedly with the tap and bug on King's premises, even though that "threat to internal security," Jack O'Dell, was no longer with King.

King, Elijah Muhammad, and Muhammad Ali were all black. (The tapping of Ali's phone is reminiscent of the Sackler play and Jack Johnson, or Jefferson, if you will.) At the 1969 Houston hearings Malcolm X's name did not crop up, apparently, or if it did, it wasn't mentioned in the press. But if King and Elijah Muhammad had *their* phones tapped and their offices bugged, it goes without saying that Malcolm's was, too.

October was also the month when the second *Newsweek* poll of 1963 was released, confirming King's status as the black leader most liked by black people. Eighty-eight percent of those polled voted for him. Jackie Robinson placed second with 80 percent, and James Meredith third, with 79 percent. Ninety-five percent of the black leadership liked King.

"Martin got up and rushed to the nearest newsstand. He had that copy of Newsweek already opened to the poll. He kept looking at it, and after a while, he must have sensed that I thought it was all disgusting, so he closed up the magazine. He pretended to be contrite. He said, 'I know I shouldn't care what they think about me. I just ought to pay it no mind and do what I must. I shouldn't be so vain.' But he was feeling good because he was first."

Person B

The year 1963 moved to its end, rumors rife that the success of the "Negro Revolution" went hand in hand with King, and indeed that seemed to be so; *Time* magazine saw it that way, and made him its Man of the Year for 1963. At that time, in a five-page essay on him, *Time* included a curious quote, attributed to King: "Segregation is the adultery of an illicit intercourse between injustice and immorality," and it "cannot be cured by the Vaseline of gradualism."

"There were two pictures. One showed me sitting on the floor beside the bathtub in which Martin sat, naked. From the angle of the photo, it looks as though I was doing something. The other photo showed me sitting on the bed beside Martin, who's laying there, nude. Now, in both cases, I was conferring with Martin in the only time available to me. Nothing, absolutely nothing took place."

Person C

The murder of Jack Kennedy both shook the members of the movement and viscerally confirmed their long-held belief that America was a murderous society. Privately, some felt that Johnson, being a Southerner, would be closer to their problems than Kennedy had been. Others, perhaps more politically realistic, knew that it would take at least two years for Johnson to erode away the Kennedy influence throughout the nation. King tended to believe in Johnson.

Thus, confident that he would be supported by the White House, Martin King went into St. Augustine that spring of 1964 to end the "moratorium" on civil rights activities that seemed to have been tacitly agreed on by all parties concerned. He went to jail in St. Augustine, of course, for that was the pattern; he and Abernathy *always* went to jail—but on their own hook, away from the hymn-singing demonstrators, almost never caught up in the mobs.

They went to jail in St. Augustine, and King came out, not to counsel the demonstrators, not to relax in Atlanta, not to meet with any biracial board that might have been forming, but to fly to New Haven and receive an honorary degree.

From that point on, the St. Augustine campaign was escalated. Cracker attorney J. B. Stoner told a white mob that, "When the Constitution said all men are created equal, it wasn't talking about niggers." Stoner was right; it wasn't. Therefore, the problem; and it continued even after President Johnson, in the presence of Martin King and others, signed the Civil Rights Act of 1964. It seemed to many that King's place was not in Johnson's office, but back in St. Augustine where compliance was only temporary.

Joanne Grant assesses the King pattern and finds it consistent in St. Augustine and other cities, beginning with Birmingham:

"He [King] shot the Birmingham Movement down with his usual technique of coming in, being the big wheel, getting the national press, and getting the President to talk to people, and sitting down and settling for a lot less than even the moderate demands. Birmingham was really the key, key one. That pattern happened in Albany, Danville, Birmingham, St. Augustine —every single place. The same pattern operated."

Miss Grant's charge seems to have been well founded in the matter of the Mississippi Freedom Democratic Party's challenge to the Credentials Committee of the National Democratic Convention that occurred during the summer of 1964.

During the Harlem Rebellion in the summer of 1964, Mayor Robert F. Wagner hastily summoned King to New York for counseling. There were many objections, Adam Powell's the loudest. King left the city, rejected by the blacks. New York City was not the South and black New Yorkers were not all that enthusiastic about his nonviolent philosophy; they were tired of the police murders of black people and particularly of young black people. A police lieutenant had shot and killed a black teen-ager, and the rebellion was on. No more praying, no more marching. King had not bothered to advise Powell or other local leaders of his invitation; rather, he glided in, like Jesus walking water, and the locals popped him pretty good.

So King retreated south. Ella Baker, who had moved from SCLC to SNCC and then to the MFDP to help them organize their challenge, asked King to tour voting centers to help build MFDP support, and he did. This was King's biggest opportunity to break out of the mold of moral suasion into something of infinitely more value—power politics.

The people in the MFDP are a tough group and undoubtedly planned to challenge the regular Democrats from their state all the way down the line. And their claim was just: Black people have never been represented in the South by Southern Congressmen, because they rarely had the vote. No one who honestly claimed to be interested in justice could deny that fact, and the time was ripe in Atlantic City in the summer of 1964 for the chips to be cashed in. The recently discovered bodies of Chaney, Goodman, and Schwerner gave the MFDP added backbone and proof of Mississippi's oppression. They thought.

In the final analysis, the workers' deaths and the murders of Herbert Lee and Medgar Evers made little difference to the Credentials Committee that met on August 22. King called for the MDFP delegates to be seated, but a compromise was in the works.

President Johnson, like any other top-ranking Democrat, did not want and could not have a rift of such dimension within the party, although there was tacit admission that the Mississippi regular delegation was improperly represented. Johnson dispatched his soon-to-be-named Vice President, Hubert Humphrey, to offer a compromise. With the help of such knowledgeable political aid-men as Tom Finney and Dave Garth,* a couple of alternate seats for MFDP were arranged

---

* Both were involved in the McCarthy campaign of 1968, and Garth works closely with Lindsay and is widely credited with helping him to achieve his victory in New York in 1969.

for. Two key members of the insurgents found the compromise acceptable. Then King—only forty-eight hours after he had demanded the seating of the MFDP delegates—about-faced and urged the other sixty-six delegates to accept the deal. Bayard Rustin urged the compromise and King went along, with the very same vigor he had previously displayed in attacking the regular delegation. King told the integrated MFDP delegates that to accept the compromise would be to make a decision that would affect the nation and the world. Favorably affect, he implied. The delegates caucused once again to consider his plea. They rejected it, holding out for the complete dismissal of the regular delegation.

Martin King should have been with them, should have been able to perceive that the enticements of Humphrey, Rustin, *et al.*, were those of the establishment and therefore meant no good for the rebel MFDP. He should have taken his cue from huge, stone-faced, red-eyed Fannie Lou Hamer, but as Joanne Grant has pointed out, black leaders did not trust the people they led, and would not listen to them. King was counting on half a loaf's being better than nothing, and that, too, had been a pattern of his: Something was better than nothing; a slight improvement was better than none at all.

Compromises that seem to favor black people have always turned out to be defeats for them: "Political expediency" is nonexistent for Negroes. *The demands made must be stood by.* King's broken-field running in the matter of the MFDP delegates caused the final, irrevocable split between SCLC and SNCC, for the youngsters had first commenced the voter registration drives and steered the MFDP into being. The realities of black life at the bottom were plain to SNCC. They tried to deal with them and with the backcountry black masses. King, on the other hand, was an urban man. And SNCC was not a one-man organization. Four different chairmen came to the fore while Martin King remained the kingpin at SCLC. SNCC saw political revolution, not moral revolution, as the key to the problem. Thus the inevitable confrontation in Atlantic City.

Although "booted out" of Atlantic City when they refused the compromise, the MFDP continued to gather documents and statistics proving (as though more proof were required) Mississippi racism in order to challenge the seating of the regular state Congressional delegation whose five members had been illegally and unconstitutionally elected. The MFDP move was effectively blocked by Omar Burelson, chairman of the House Administration Committee in January, 1965, as King, fresh from Scandinavia, was mounting the Selma March. Eight months later, by a vote of 228 to 143, the House of Representatives finally dismissed the MFDP challenge.

The issue was completely misjudged by King. The evidence of the unconstitutionality of Mississippi voting restrictions against blacks was massive, historical, and undeniable. King's continued full-time interest, his prestige, could have forced through a wedge; he could have mounted a nationwide protest. But he did not see the forest for the trees; he blew his greatest opportunity to deal with the tangible.

Less than a year later, black power, rather than nonviolence, caught the public eye, and its origin can be traced to Atlantic City when King switched allegiances. King's fumble, however, led to the strengthening of black political groups in the South and to an escalation of voter registration activity. The result has been, in county and local elections, that black candidates have won, and are winning still, offices that have been closed to them since the end of Reconstruction. (Now the Nixon Administration appears to desire to bring a halt to the trend by easing school desegregation orders and softening the Voting Rights Act of 1966.) *

We sat in The Tavern on the Green in New York City's Central Park. It was toward the end of September, 1964. "It

* On March 24, 1970, Nixon stated that his administration would work to wipe out *de jure* segregation, but could do little about *de facto* segregation, missing the point that *de jure* segregation was the creator of *de facto* segregation.

was tough in Atlantic City. While Humphrey and Rustin worked on King, we worked through the rank-and-file of those people from MFDP. We had to keep the whole goddamn convention from blowing up. They were tough people. King was easy."

A Democratic Party public relations man

Nineteen

NINETEEN sixty-four was also the year when rumors made the rounds that King was in line to receive the Nobel Prize, the award for pursuing peace.

The tense situation between King and Adam Powell over King's attempt to grandstand at the Harlem Rebellion of the summer had eased. King not only preached in Powell's church, but visited him on the island of milk and Scotch, Bimini. Perhaps he should have stayed on the island, for when he returned to the mainland, he went to a meeting with J. Edgar Hoover who, in a Washington press conference in November, 1964, had called King "the most notorious liar in the country." The meeting had been designed to end differences between the two men.

King biographers generally agree that Hoover's statement had come as a response to what King had said about FBI agents during the Albany campaign two years before. Hoover's remark has been printed over and over again, but what elicited it has not been set down. It almost seems to have been uttered as a *non sequitur*. King himself said, "What motivated such an irresponsible accusation is a mystery to me."

Only one answer makes sense. Hoover simply was not referring to the Albany campaign.

"A Chicago columnist, Mike Royko, reported not long ago that a former F.B.I. agent took him out and tried to disclose some private facts about Martin Luther King, Jr., which had

196

no bearing on his ability to lead the civil rights movement and no legal relevance whatsoever. Nor did these disclosures bear in any way on national security. The facts were disclosed in an apparent effort to embarrass King's leadership and diminish his standing with the press. Royko did not run the F.B.I.'s gossip."

The Nation, October 27, 1969

John Edgar Hoover, who has served under ten Presidents, is not now and never has been a friend of the civil rights movement. Trial balloons proclaiming the possibility of his retirement have been sent up from time to time, but quickly hauled down. President Johnson waived his mandatory retirement; he is now a very ripe seventy-four. Black people, and I would imagine a good number of white people as well, assume that Hoover has served for so long simply because he must know a lot about a lot of people, things they would not be happy to see made public.

(A former Senate aide told me that once while attending a meeting of a group of Senators, there was a serious discussion about forming a task force to go into Hoover's office, should he die suddenly, and remove the files. Presumably this was to prevent Hoover's successor from using the information the files contained.)

Anyway, they met, King and Hoover. What really transpired may never be known. *Newsweek* reported of that meeting that "King explained that a statement attributed to him last summer (in which he was quoted as having warned Negroes not to report civil rights violations to the F.B.I. because the agents were unsympathetic to the Negroes' cause) had been inaccurately reported."

Thus, in the parlance of the streets, King copped out. King gave Hoover a chance to counter with a similar cop-out, but he was in charge, and *Newsweek* went on to say, "Hoover ignored the opportunity to apologize thus presented to him. . . ."

At the meeting King was reportedly given assurances that the murderers of Chaney, Goodman, and Schwerner were about to be apprehended. Outside the director's office King said, "There must not be misunderstanding between the F.B.I. and civil rights leaders," and concluded that there had been an "amicable discussion."

After that visit with Hoover, King prepared for his journey to Scandinavia, to Oslo, where he would indeed receive the Nobel Prize. There followed in London, Oslo, and Stockholm, days and nights of pomp and ceremony; hours filled with meeting people, holding press conferences, and discussing the racial situation back in the United States.

People found King most impressive. For King, it was a high moment, and he had come very far. He led his black delegation of thirty-odd people into practically all-white Scandinavia, took its top prize, and left.

All did not go well in Scandinavia.

"I was sleeping when they called me from downstairs and said that I had to come down to the desk at once. I pulled on my robe and went down. The police were there with a woman later said to be the biggest whore in town. And they had caught her coming out of the hotel with watches and wallets belonging to some of the people in our party. Well, she was there. There had been other women running through the hotel like chickens without their heads, looking for Martin. And all the guys were putting it to them that, if the girls gave them some pussy first, they'd see that she got to Martin. The whore? I thought it better to let her go with everything she had rather than embarrass ourselves and our hosts."

Person C

"I thought you might be interested because of the book you're working on. I just came back from Washington where I heard about the tapes. Couple of guys told me about them:

—— *of* ——, —— *of* ——, *and—well, everybody in the press corps has heard about them or had them played for them by the FBI guys. These are from Stockholm. Pictures too, man. The whole works."*

A Reporter

From Stockholm, Dr. and Mrs. King went to Paris. One night, very tired but happy to be away from the press, they sat in one of the coldest corners of LeRoy Haynes' soul food restaurant on Rue Clauzel. Haynes, a big, sometimes jovial black man, a Negro college All-American football player in his younger days, an ex-GI of World War II, a character actor in French film and television, later told me about that night.

"They were sitting in that corner you just left because it was too cold, sitting there, having a nice quiet time. I got a call. Some brother in a hotel on George Fifth was having a party. He wanted me to cook up a mess of chitlins and fry some chicken and take it over there. Then I started figuring out loud: I have to cook the stuff, get a cab, ride it all the way over to the sixteenth and then get a cab coming back here. Well, Dr. King, he said, 'LeRoy, just cook it up. We'll drop it off. We have to go over that way anyhow.' That's what I did, and he carried the food over for me."

The Nobel Prize was still fresh in his hip pocket. Newsmen had been dogging him ever since word came that the murderers of Chaney, Goodman, and Schwerner had been arrested. But there was King and his wife, and I see them now, riding that cab out of the third, going through Les Halles onto Rue du Pont Neuf, swerving them to Rue de Rivoli, past Place de la Concorde to the Champs Elysées, steaming hot chitlins and hard-fried chicken resting in aluminum pots in their laps. (Chitlins came originally from France.) I like to think of Martin King that way.

Once back home there were lukewarm honors accorded to King, but mostly, no honors at all. The honors at home didn't really matter; he'd won the prize, and there weren't many other Americans who could lay claim to that. Besides, back in Alabama, things were brewing again.

"Selma was the sell-out of the century," a black reporter says. His opinion is shared by many.

People think back to Alabama and seem to conclude that King had been a victor in the civil rights battles that took place in that state. There had been the Montgomery boycott, the Freedom Rides, and the Birmingham campaign, but as Louis Lomax has put it, King "left . . . his work undone."

In his book on Sammy Younge, James Forman reports that King and SCLC were to have concentrated on Alabama in a voter registration plan in 1964, together with SNCC. But King, who "wasn't too good at that kind of work, that knocking on the doors," went to St. Augustine instead. But by the end of 1964 SCLC was again playing the idea of a voter registration campaign back in Alabama. According to Forman, SCLC's interest stemmed directly from the encouragement of the National Democratic Party. President Johnson had not carried several Southern states in the election and, like the Kennedys before John's death, felt that pulling the up-till-then-unwanted black man into a voting situation would add new strength to the Democrats.

SNCC, already established in Selma, once again joined SCLC in the venture, "But disagreement on such key issues as concepts of leadership, working methods, and organizing voters for independent political action versus Democratic Party politics, bred conflict between SNCC and SCLC staffs in Alabama," Forman writes.

It is of course easy now to pose King's lack of foresight in the MFDP case in Atlantic City against the voter registration drive in Selma. But his position in Selma would have been tremendously stronger had he returned to the South not on the side of the Democratic National Committee, but on the side of the millions of black people who had been denied the ballot.

Forman describes working with SCLC as "frustrating," and

others through the years agreed. "You can't get *decisions* from those people; no answers, no decisions." SNCC voted against participation in the big march from Selma to Montgomery, but asked individuals to go along if they wished.

"Then we heard that Dr. King would not appear at the march he himself had called," Forman writes. "Without his newsworthy presence, it seemed likely that the lives of many black people would be even more endangered."

King, who'd been in Washington conferring with President Johnson, returned to Selma and was "persuaded" not to lead the demonstration himself on the seventh of March. It seems to have been "SCLC policy" that the leaders not be arrested in the opening phases of a campaign, but that policy seems to have been pliable; King and Abernathy were usually arrested, made themselves available for arrest before the masses became genuinely organized, as in Albany, Birmingham, and St. Augustine.

Although SNCC leaders tried repeatedly to contact King from Atlanta, they could get no response; they wished to know *why* King was not leading the march, why Hosea Williams and John Lewis were in the vanguard instead

King's response to the clubbings at Pettus Bridge was, "If I had known it was going to be like that I'd have gone myself." Which was what the people from SNCC had been driving at all along.

Almost at once another march was called for Tuesday, March 9. The federal court of the middle district intervened, offering instead to hold hearings rather than allow the second march. James Forman describes what then followed:

"Martin Luther King decided to accept the Judge's condition. The march would be postponed.

"The entire group left immediately for Brown's Chapel in Selma. There, to my amazement, King pledged before a mass meeting that the march would begin the next morning at eight o'clock!"

The SNCC people were confused and angry. It seemed to them that King was deliberately misleading the people, saying one thing to them and quite another to the white power structure. Then the pipe to Washington was opened up, King to Katzenbach, LeRoy Collins to King, back and forth, with Katzenbach reportedly very angry. Why was he angry? Why, anyway, was King calling him?

Eight the next morning. The people were assembled once again. Those who had been served with papers forbidding them to march by federal injunction were advised not to march; there were only three. The group moved off. In the gray morning distance beyond the bridge were the troopers, troopers who only two days before had crushed the marchers to the ground. Fifteen hundred strong, the marchers approached, King, this time, in the lead. Several supporters from the North had joined this march, among them some prominent people like the wife of Senator Paul Douglas and the widow of Harold Ickes, former Secretary of the Interior.

A few feet from the troopers, King called the marchers to a halt, and they knelt in prayer, and he then enjoined them to return back across the bridge. Forman: "Needless to say, people were dismayed, baffled and angry."

A deal, another deal had been made, but King had not informed those who had been prepared to absorb another beating. During the hearing in federal court, Judge Frank Johnson asked King, "Is it correct to say that when you started across the bridge you knew at that time you did not intend to march to Montgomery?"

King replied, "Yes, it is. There was a tacit agreement at the bridge that we would go no further."

Rather than having been made "at the bridge," that tacit agreement appears to have been made elsewhere, perhaps on the telephone. There had been barely concealed contempt for King and his methods on the part of the younger, more realistic people, and even a number of whites at that time were forced to raise their eyebrows. The New York *Times* for March 10 noted that, "Many of these spokesmen privately charged that King had betrayed them by his behind-the-scenes bargaining."

Why did King have to bargain? Forman notes that before this incident, he hoped that "events might continue to move [King] away from the U.S. government." He was disappointed then. Like many, many people, he wondered why in hell it was necessary to advise Washington of every plan.

"Hey, [laughter] we got a funny story on Martin Luther King last week. The midwest, somewhere. He had to leave a place in a hurry, his pants in his hands."

"You're not going to run that are you? You can't run that."

"Oh, hell no. Just stick it in the files somewhere. With the other stories."

"Yeah." The best stories are the ones the newspapers and newsmagazines never run. The reporters titillate themselves reading and rereading them, and you can never get to many files until they have been "brushed," cleaned of material fit for no eyes but theirs.

Conversation (with commentary) with a
newsmagazine reporter

Ultimately there came out of the Selma campaign a Voting Rights Act, the registration of hundreds of thousands of blacks and, subsequently, the emergence of black elected officials. But, the United States Civil Rights Commission indirectly underlined King's failures in Alabama in 1955, 1963, and 1965. The commission had convened its first hearings there in 1958. Ten years later it returned, and in a second investigation covering 16 Alabama counties, revealed that three-fifths of the 360,000 people living in those counties were black, earning a median annual income of $1,279. This "progress" was tartly measured by Paul Good in his *Cycle to Nowhere*, U.S. Civil Rights Commission Clearinghouse Publication number 14.

"The testimony belongs in the 1958 transcript yet it is down in black and white, date 1968."

But that report was still to come when the Selma campaign was finished. If there had been rumors about King's back room wheeling and dealing with government officials before, it was certainly now accepted fact that *something* was going on.

Even so, King now cast his eyes up from the South and pledged to take his nonviolent campaign into the North—into the North where the National Urban League and the NAACP had built strongholds over the decades. SCLC had been designed specifically to do *in the South* what the other civil rights organizations had been trying to do in the North. His intrusion into the Northern citadel of Harlem had been met with extreme hostility. There was a lesson to be learned there, and King did not learn it. He would be rebuffed in Los Angeles, too, not only by white officials, but by the people in Watts who had witnessed or participated in the grim events of their rebellion.

In Chicago, King had an ally, the Reverend Jesse Jackson, a handsome, self-confident former salesman and head of the Northern division of SCLC's almost unheralded Operation Breadbasket. (Jackson has had considerable success since King's death, and has been thought by many to be the man who will replace Ralph Abernathy as head of SCLC.)

Of course, the word went out before King moved north that he was coming, so there was ample time for the Chicago power structure to prepare itself.

Lomax declares that King's campaign was "doomed from the onset." It (Chicago) "was Martin's first, and last, campaign outside the South. It was his first big effort to stave off the black violence then spreading across the republic; it was his final stand against black power. . . . Chicago was final evidence that *The System* that controls the ghetto would not yield power to the nonviolent and the civilized."

It is Lomax's contention, along with many, many others,

that King failed to realize how deeply entrenched corruption, vice, and crime were in Chicago, and how firmly intertwined: "I was surprised, and honestly so, that Martin did not disappear into Lake Michigan, his feet encased in concrete. For this is the precise fate of those who threaten the nickel and dime numbers racket that rakes in millions of welfare client dollars each year."

There is a contradiction here, for Lomax seems to be saying that King appealed to the black underclasses at this point in his life. But Lomax also said that King did not understand the guts of ghetto life. We know that he did not really deal with it.

What *is* clear about the Chicago campaign was that the widest variety of forces were ranged against him. No doubt the criminal element which so often works hand in hand with the law enforcement agencies stood against him too. The most obvious pressure against his being in Chicago came from powerful community elements, those that stood on the side of law and order.

I make the assumption that if Mike Royko of the Chicago *Daily News* was approached by a former FBI man, other people in the Chicago area were as well, with news of King's "indiscretions." The gossip could have been efficiently utilized by Mayor Daley's office, by newsmen opposed to King's presence in town, by certain influential blacks who saw alignment with King as a liability—which could have been precisely why they were advised of the gossip. Brother Brightness indicated in the earlier pages of this book that Roman Catholic officials might have valued the information most of all, and could have been the first to have received it.

The shooting of James Meredith in Mississippi probably gave King an opportunity to break away from an icy Chicago with dignity, an undeniably perfect excuse. That shooting, ironically enough, brought him to the Lorraine Motel for conferences with other black leaders who'd met there to take up the march for Meredith. The South was King's milieu; there they outright called him a nigger, a troublemaker, a Communist, and daily threatened to kill him. These attitudes ran from the bottom of the community right on through the top, and no one smiled and shook his hand one moment only to curse him the next. The North was an enigma to him in many ways. Much of the SCLC support came from the North, but he did not seem to understand that Northern money meant that he was to stay away from the North.

King feared the phrase "black power" the way people fear a truth they are not ready to hear. A power that was all black eliminated whites and, quite probably, their contributions; an all-black power negated King's concept of an all-Christian love that went beyond the color of one's skin. But the rapidity with which the phrase gained acceptance in the black communities, and the venality with which it was described in the white communities indicated that its meaning and validity were clearly understood by all.

Martin King must have been a tired man on that march. He had fled the powerful, secret machinations of black and white, political and religious forces in Chicago, only to discover as he moved along the Mississippi highway in shirt-sleeves and broad-brimmed hat, that he had lost the young blacks, too. There had emerged a new philosophy of the Negro people, one that had been scratching the roots of the Northern ghettos for generations, but had had its greatest impact in the South. That philosophy was black power.

Like so many of us, King in his speeches took on the sketchings of black power. He used "Negro" and "black people" interchangeably; black became beautiful, although his secret distaste for black women remained constant. He hedged on being forthrightly opposed to the black rebellions.

Perhaps, just perhaps, the answer to the meaning of his presence here could be answered by his opposition to the war. As King saw it, there was a direct relationship between the war in Southeast Asia and racism at home. Vietnam could draw him closer to the antiwar whites he was losing with the advent of black power, and make black people think not only about racism at home, but how it was practiced abroad. This, then, could be, and was, King's finest hour, the hour truly fitting a winner of the Nobel Peace Prize.

Twenty

"MARTIN and the rest of them had a code. A very attractive woman was called 'Doctor.' I forget the other names for women not so attractive."
"What were you called?"
"I was a 'Doctor.'"

Person B

The *Washington Post,* Wednesday, June 11, 1969
Laurence Stern and Richard Harwood
"KING TAPE" EMERGES FROM LEGEND TO UNDERLINE A DANGER TO LIBERTIES

"For *several years* [italics added] a piece of Washington apocrypha known as 'the Martin Luther King tape' was the subject of sly and ugly surmise among certain journalistic insiders. There are those who claim to have had The Tape played for them by obliging law enforcement officials. Others are said to have been given transcripts of a gathering, bugged by Government investigators, at which Dr. King and friends were present."

"There is love as *libido* which is the movement of the needy toward that which fulfills the need. There is love as *philia* which is movement of the equal toward union with the equal. There is love as *eros* which is the movement of that which is lower in power and meaning to that which is higher. In all three of these forms of love the element of desire is present.

But there is a form of love which transcends these, namely, the desire to fulfill the longing of the other being. This is love as *agape*. All love, except *agape*, is dependent on contingent characteristics which change and are partial, such as repulsion and attraction, passion and sympathy. *Agape* is independent of these states. It affirms the other unconditionally. It is *agape* that suffers and forgives. It seeks the personal fulfillment of the other."

Martin Luther King, Jr.
Doctoral thesis

I will make another assumption. King, like nearly everyone at SCLC headquarters, says a reporter, "was vaguely aware of FBI plants in the movement." At some point along the way, someone in government let him know that he had been taped and photographed in situations that might be considered compromising by the puritan masses. He was asked to soft-pedal his activities, to make the appearance of carrying on as usual when in substance, he would not be. Further assumption: King went along with the program to some extent. Selma appears to be the most obvious case in point. The criticism and the name-calling jarred him. He had to question his rightful role of a leader of black people; he could not remain compromised. At stake was more than his personal reputation and that of his family. It would take a very strong man to see and admit that. The stake was the success of the movement and all it meant not only to black Americans, but to all Americans, for, as the French Tunisian writer Albert Memmi writes, "every colonial nation carries the seeds of fascist temptation in its bosom."

It seems to me that King broke with whatever compromise he might have made when he jumped into the Vietnam War protest, determined to sock it to those who would have restrained him. And when he made his decision, he must have known that his life, although he had been threatened time and time again, was now measured.

By early 1967 King, who had once enjoyed being listed in the popularity polls, was no longer among the top ten. In the White House he had been replaced by Dr. Joseph Jackson of Chicago. The Martin Luther King of Montgomery, 1955, of Birmingham, 1963, and of the March on Washington, was in a slow, calculated decline, and the June, 1967, rebellions in Newark and Detroit didn't help. Of course, the press asked him to comment on them, but it is worth noting that King did not rush in, as he had in Watts or Harlem; he kept his distance.

Somewhere within this man who liked the competitiveness of sports, who once carried a gun, who tolerated bodyguards, who could not be sure that if his wife were attacked he could remain nonviolent, an explosion must have occurred. He could state flatly that he remained convinced of the efficacy of non-violence, even in the face of overwhelming offensive violence. But he could also say (*Time to Break Silence*): "These are revolutionary times. All over the globe men are revolting against old systems of exploitation and oppression and out of the wombs of a frail world new systems of justice and equality are being born. The shirtless and barefoot people of the land are rising up as never before. 'The people who sat in darkness have seen a great light.' We in the West must support these revolutions."

He must have known that for the people of the United States to support revolutions abroad, they would first have to support the "black revolution" at home, and that our failure to support the ones overseas had a great deal to do with the suppression of the one at home.

King rapped in Riverside Church the night of April 4, 1967. Black men who deal in foreign policy for whatever reasons are not well liked either here at home or abroad. One thinks back to men like William Monroe Trotter, W. E. B. DuBois; to Marcus Garvey, although he wasn't in the same class; to Malcolm X, who was learning as he went; their fates were distressingly similar, perhaps suspiciously similar. Exile, accidental death, assassination. . . .

It is natural to believe that the more King became a thorn in the government's side because of Vietnam, the more intense became the pressure for him to withdraw under the threat of exposure. The press, most of which by now had been advised in one way or another of the King away from the pulpit, soft-pedaled their coverage on him. His *Time to Break Silence* talk, for example, was poorly reported. But his *faux pas* in approving the use of police force in Newark and Detroit was widely covered.

This last, however, came at a time when most black people were convinced, and with good reason, that nothing King could say could dispute the fact that the police were in business to annihilate them. That King made the remark at all is another example of how he could, when the pressure was really on, vacillate with remarkably poor results.

To the Vietnam issue, on the other hand, he came with a certainty that must have made some people realize that his symbol could with the right breaks, actually become a genuine power to contend with. He was, after all, considered to be a possible running mate on a peace ticket with Dr. Spock (and we all know what happened to Dr. Spock). Most threatening of all was King's planned Poor People's March, for a person who seeks to unite the nation's poor across caste and class lines may have the ingredient for genuinely altering the society. Like others before him, he is a danger; he must go.

The powers that tend to be secret believed they had him compromised. We must deal with that to be able to grasp the depth of the games that are being played with legitimate human aspirations whether they be for the elimination of racism or of Vietnam as a battlefield.

I. F. Stone writes (June 30, 1969): "While the excuse for tapping King's phones was 'internal security' its chief result was to permit the FBI to spread stories about King's sex life.

"Carl Rowan in his column (*Washington Star,* June 15) said 'FBI officials were going before Congressional committees and partly justifying larger appropriations by titillating some Congressmen' with 'tid-bits' picked up through wiretaps and buggings. In 1964 and 1965 as head of the U.S. Information Agency, Rowan had access to these FBI reports. 'I know how much dirt the FBI has dug up,' he wrote in a second column June 20, 'and 90 per cent of it is barnyard gossip that has nothing to do with 'internal security' or 'Marxist influences.'

". . . Hoover first leaked word that Robert Kennedy had authorized a King wiretap during the Oregon primary last year. Hoover hated both men. In an interview with the *Washington Star,* June 19, Hoover again blamed Kennedy and attributed the tap to King's 'Marxist ideas and associations.' Hoover would like to see King and Kennedy assassinated again, this time morally."

In their column in the Washington *Post* on June 11, Stern and Harwood ask: ". . . Why was Dr. King under surveillance? No one has said. . . . It is also ironic that this seemingly gratuitous invasion of Dr. King's personal life occurred at a time when many high-ranking members of the Justice Department would have expressed nothing less than roaring outrage at the thought that his phone was being tapped by Government agents. . . ."

So many, then, thought King was in the bag.

A black man, I do not have to ask why such "barnyard gossip" was never circulated about the alleged, red-hot romance between Robert Kennedy and Marilyn Monroe. Why should I ask after the alleged extracurricular activities of John F. Kennedy or Dwight D. Eisenhower or Prince Philip or Princess Margaret? Why do I understand so perfectly that they could not break Adam Powell with repeated disclosures of his sexual proclivities, and thus, finally, had to refuse him, on no grounds at all, his seat from Congress?

Anything black people get into motion is going to be monitored, anything, and then, if possible, compromised. That is the way things go in this nation; they always have. They are just worse now, so bad that Chet Huntley on NBC radio on July 11, 1969, said that most United States Senators go about their daily routines certain that their phones are tapped.

About three weeks after King was murdered, the New York *Times* (May 25, 1968) reported "that it was commonly felt by everyone, including Dr. King, that their phones were tapped." Ralph Abernathy "said that Dr. King and his aides frequently joked about being 'bugged' by the Federal Bureau of Investigation."

So King, at the very *least*, suspected that he was under surveillance. At what point did he receive, without return address, a print, perhaps of a tape recording or a copy of a photograph, that definitely told him that he had been put in the trick?

Only in a society that fears, secretly exalts sex, and holds puritanical views about it could the political blackmail of Martin King have been possible. Nor were the agencies responsible the only ones involved; the press that reached down into the South and created King and then extolled his list of dubious victories turns out to have been a co-conspirator. It is true that it did not record stories about the tapes or photographs while King lived. It only knew about them—which was enough—for they backed away from him, turned the glare of their annihilating publicity on others. Few, I believe, and none that I know of, publicly bared the political blackmail going on during King's life. Now, it seems to me, they are all castigating the FBI while they, by maintaining their silence, became partners in both the breaking of King and the attempted destruction of a movement for which they once seemed to hold great esteem.

Toward his end, like so many of us whose ends have not yet come, King seemed to turn ever so slightly back (or should it be for the first time?) to his people. He gave the Centennial Address at the International Cultural Evening on the 100th birthday of the late W. E. B. Du Bois. This was February 28,

1968. It is strange that he returned to Du Bois then, practically on the eve of his death; it is also strange to contemplate that Du Bois died the evening before the March on Washington in 1963. Du Bois might have agreed with King about *Zeitgeist;* there *was* something in the air, something in the spirit of the times that reached beyond their differences which were political and religious, to bind them together in circumstance.

At that Carnegie Hall meeting, King said in his closing remarks, speaking of the Poor People's March:

"We have to go to Washington because they have declared an armistice in the war on poverty while squandering billions to expand a senseless, cruel, unjust war in Vietnam. We will go there, we will demand to be heard, and we will stay until the administration responds. If this means the forcible repression of our movement, we will confront it, for we have done this before. If this means scorn or ridicule, we will embrace it for that is what America's poor now receive. If it means jail we accept it willingly, for the millions of poor already are imprisoned by exploitation and discrimination."

One hundred and twenty-five SCLC staff people were not nearly enough to drum up the forces for the Spring Protest— the Poor Peoples' March. But that had always been an inherent weakness of SCLC. In conception PPM was a grand thing, massive, powerful, demanding. Internally, it was a shambles, for there were too many sharp staff differences. But, as there had been more than one March on Washington, it was conceivable that there could be more than just the PPM of 1968. It was not the numbers, 50,000, that caused unhappiness in secret, high places, but the idea, the very idea of assembling the poor of all races.

Of course, Martin King never saw the march; he was cut down in Memphis. But what has been the result of his plan for getting it together? An upsurge of American Indian nationalism ("Custer Got What He Deserved"); a powerful Mexican-American labor coalition in the West and Southwest; a new sense of recognition now felt by welfare recipients.

History will record that King gave initial impetus to many individuals and groups that still attack the structure of this society. The King nonviolent example in Montgomery led to the peaceful sit-ins and the formation of SNCC. SNCC began the voter registration drives with such earnestness that they resulted, finally, in the election of black local and state representatives in numbers nearing those of the black officials during Reconstruction. From SNCC too came the Lowndes County Freedom Party that evolved into the Black Panthers who are now being systematically decimated by the police and the courts. But they have already inspired the formation of other black radical groups and set an example now being followed by young radical whites.

Also out of SNCC came James Forman, now head of the Black Economic Development Conference, which has shaken the American churches as King never did with his Black Manifesto, demanding that the churches pay reparation to black people for their prolonged status as slaves and second-class citizens.

Through Jesse Jackson, Operation Breadbasket in Chicago has become SCLC's "economic wing." Jackson has run head on into the local labor unions, and what he is demanding from them for black workers within the construction industry is a very far cry from what King even conceived in that area.

King's position in the Vietnam protest movement is incontestable; he was there during its "middle period," 1966, and a part of its growth can be laid to his interest and presence. His widow has carried on; indeed she was involved in it before he was. We have seen that protest increase in numbers and intensity until it became a groundswell capable, at least in some measure, of forcing Lyndon Johnson not to run again as President. It drove the administration to make concessions and adjustments in the draft system, to announce troop withdrawals, and to sit down to the peace table in Avenue Kleber in Paris.

In short, then, Martin King in great part is responsible for the racial, moral, political, and economic polarizations now gravely affecting the nation. His murder did not eliminate but germinated the trends with which we now deal. His very lacks and flaws made others determined to do away with them in themselves. His failure to achieve moral gains made others see that the gains could only be political. His nouveau middle-class background first attracted the young, themselves driving toward middle-class status, and then turned them from pre-occupation with that to leadership of the masses. Coming from a home where the father dominated and the mother assumed almost equal power, King could not evolve into a father figure himself but remained at heart a youngster. In relation to the young blacks of SNCC he was weak, if not altogether a failure, as a father figure who did not command their respect. King appears to have been unable to make decisions and stick to them; his vacillations were commonplace. Nor could he tolerate competition. Witness his inability or refusal to allow SCLC to grow, his refusal to accept strong and willful men to serve beside him, a factor that must reflect back on his child-hood with his father. If he did not allow them to serve with him, he would never have to cope with a confrontation.

He was prone to the weaknesses of many men who are basically unsure of themselves; he could not delegate power or authority. He had to be on the scene himself. He was vain in the manner of many who have been acclaimed by sources and forces about which he should have held the deepest suspicion, but he was a man of immense charm and of positive beliefs, although he could not always act on them.

This was the makeup of the small pudgy man who was Martin Luther King. He lived in his time and by design and accident made himself a force beyond it. He was killed, murdered in a conspiracy that may never be proved. Louis Lomax believes that it involved Southern businessmen. This might be true. A conspiracy of this kind could involve almost anyone, but surely Martin King, for all his weaknesses, was killed because behind those weaknesses lay profound strengths.

All talk of conspiracy in his death seems to have quieted down —even though the man accused of killing him publicly refused to rule out a conspiracy.

The thing for conspirators and conspirators-to-be to remember is that there will always come along another Cinqué, another Gabriel, another John Brown, another Nat Turner, another Martin King. The chain must have many links, and Martin King was but one of them.

There are those who believe that by murdering the link of the moment, they can sever the chain; then there are those who say, if we do not honor that link the chain is finished. And so, in September, 1969, the story was broken that a memorial to Martin King, a proposal that at first was greeted with enthusiasm by President Nixon, had been abandoned. The King family had become disenchanted with the attitude— one of "growing indifference" to the memorial—of not only the President, but of his aides. All this was after administration officials and architects had been in direct contact with Mrs. Martin Luther King, Jr., who said, "We felt that to get Federal support for a memorial would have been a beautiful thing not only for our country but for oppressed people throughout the world. But President Nixon's attitude, his lack of real concern, suggests that his administration is motivated by racist attitudes."

It seems to me that we already have a memorial, living and vigorous, to Martin King. No doubt, he would have liked the monument; it would have appealed to his vanity. It would have appealed to what seems to be a family vanity. No matter, his memorial is secure; not a marble slab rising up from the Morehouse College campus, but a *presence* in the hearts of those who can no longer, must no longer dream of overcoming on the simple base of morality.

J. Edgar Hoover is closer to Attorney General John Mitchell than he was to Robert Kennedy or Ramsey Clark. The gossip about King has gathered more force during the Nixon Administration than it ever did under Kennedy and Johnson. The King family, unfortunately but inexcusably, was guilty of remarkable naïveté for them when it sought administration help in putting up the memorial.

In matters pertaining to Richard Nixon, King had mixed feelings, which were revealed in response to a query by Earl Mazo in September, 1958. Mazo was then with the Washington Bureau of the New York *Herald Tribune*. Naïveté, mingled with suspicion, is evident; and it is clear that King had an eye on the elections of 1960.

Mazo wrote:

> I'm writing a book about Vice President Nixon at the request of Harper and Brothers, the publishers. It will be an objective biography through Mr. Nixon's sixth year as Vice President, and I am seeking information from all available sources. I would be grateful if you would write me your observations of and any information you may have about Mr. Nixon. I would particularly appreciate your evaluation of him, any anecdotes regarding him that you know or have heard and your best guess about his political future. Thank you for your kindness.

In reply, King said that he did not know Nixon as well as many others but had had some personal dealings with him. King cautiously suggested that his appraisal could not, therefore, be the best. Then he struck out, admitting that he had been "strongly opposed" to the Vice President before he met him. A major reason for this opposition was Nixon's stand against Helen Gahagan Douglas. Further, King found Nixon's voting record, which tended to side with the "right wing of the Republican party," distasteful.

King held the hope that it was possible for Nixon to have experienced a complete change, mostly because of his travels around the world. During his tours, King suggested, it became clear to Nixon just how much the tensions over race in the United States had hurt the prestige of the country among other nations.

Quite naïvely, I think, Nixon's being a Quaker gave King the faith that basically he was a right-thinking man—perhaps even more right-thinking than Eisenhower. Martin King, rather shakily, pursued the ghost that, had Nixon been President in 1954, he would have done more than Ike to supplement the Supreme Court's decision of that year.

King is one of the few people who found Nixon to be a "personable" man and the possessor of one of the "most magnetic personalities" he'd ever met. But King also felt that such a personality could be dangerous if used for political expediency.

On the trip to Africa to celebrate Ghana's independence, King watched Nixon closely and thought him to be an excellent diplomat, with a good sense of timing and of what to say. King claimed that most of the reporters began the trip disliking Nixon intensely, but by the end of it, most had completely reversed their opinions of the Vice President.

Nixon seemed far and away removed from the man who made the Checkers speech in 1952 to save himself from political oblivion.

Finally, King said, "And so I would conclude by saying that if Richard Nixon is not sincere, he is the most dangerous man in America."

As Richard Nixon was pushing his way into Ebenezer Baptist Church, the King church in Atlanta, for King's funeral, several black people hooted at him and shouted, "Opportunist." "That cat's just looking for votes," someone muttered scornfully.

While King lived, Nixon was cool toward him, toward the movement. At his death, like other notables, he went to the funeral and later indicated that he wished to go further in honoring King. Then he turned his back on the project. Some say it was because of his "Southern strategy." But the Republicans have always had a "Southern strategy"; today it seems to be working.

King must have twisted and turned in his coffin. He had lived during a time when it was possible to appeal to the government to right the wrongs of history and the American nation. And he had appealed, time and time again, through the courts, through personal conferences with Presidents, through moral suasion. But the terror of the present time has not trickled down completely to the people. For there *is* terror when you consider that now the government sides with the opposition that King tilted with for thirteen years. There *is* terror when the government seeks to revise voting rights with the full knowledge that whatever its spokesmen say that revision will be bad news for blacks; there *is* terror when some have accused the government, along with local and state agencies of practicing genocide on that radical step-brood of King's, the Black Panthers. King himself must have come to know that terror when it sought to compromise him. The full force of it struck him that cool spring night on the balcony of the Lorraine Motel.

He had been made to fail in his approaches. More realistic approaches are being blocked, bought off, derailed. To what Constitutional, to what moral authority do the black, the poor, and the young now appeal? This book is basically addressed to that point. Black aspirations move in a basic vacuum, in an arena of hypocrisy. None of us, black or interested-involved white, should forget, not for an instant, that equality with all its ringing echoes is an alien, if not an altogether empty, premise in these United States. Always was, always will be in the eyes of many people. Talking about it is one thing; but we are not to mistake talking about it for really doing something to achieve it. Equality would "ruin" the nation or, at the very least, turn it around. History is the immutable proof, is the only witness required to bear this out.

There is no reliable authority then for us to appeal to. Martin King was no saint, but would a saint have fared better?

They speak of anarchy coming from the Left to obscure the fact that there already exists a genteel anarchy in the Middle and on the Right; otherwise would there not be a reliable authority to appeal to?

Perhaps now it is time to return to a theme of King's that once echoed feebly throughout the country. It is the one about an unjust law being no law at all, and thus unworthy of being observed. Widen that to authority. In his doctoral thesis—how wise we often are when we are young!—King wrote what many have come to believe:

"... Reliable authority simply conserves and hands on to others what has been found to be true by some other test than authority. In other words, the trustworthiness of what is found in an authority does not depend upon the authority ... authority like revelation depends on some further test of truth."

On, perhaps, the black people of the United States of America and now, without Martin Luther King, Jr.